SURVIVE THE
COMING STORM

SURVIVE THE COMING STORM

THE VALUE OF A PREPAREDNESS LIFESTYLE

RAY GANO

DEFENDER

CRANE

Survive the Coming Storm
The Value of a Preparedness Lifestyle

Defender
Crane, Missouri 65633
©2011 by Ray Gano
All rights reserved. Published 2011
Printed in the United States of America.
ISBN: 9780983621621

A CIP catalog record of this book is available from the Library of Congress.
Cover illustration and design by Shim Franklin.
All Scripture references are taken from the Authorized King James Version.

Dedication

I would like to dedicate this book to the two most important people in my life:

First, to my Lord and Savior Jesus Christ, who saved me from my sins, and in Him I give my life daily.

And to my wife, Tracye, who inspires me to greatness, all the while remaining humble. I love her with all my heart and could not ask for better soul mate than her. *I love you!*

A note to my reader: Always remember, TRUE warriors fight not because they hate what is in front of them, but because they love what is behind them.

I love my country; it is still the greatest country in the world to live in. God's Word states that there is a time and a season for all things. Our nation is heading into one of those times and seasons. But we need to remember that this is just a storm, and our nation will come out on the other side. Our nation goes through the fires of purification about every one hundred years. We have made it in the past; we will make it through this storm. God will not forsake this country. We may get a good chastising, but we will not be forsaken. God bless America!

Psalms 144:1: "Blessed be the LORD my strength, which teacheth my hands to war, and my fingers to fight."

Luke 22:36: "Then said he unto them, But now, he that hath a purse, let him take it, and likewise his scrip: and he that hath no sword, let him sell his garment, and buy one."

Contents

Ray Gano

GROWING UP WITH A PREPAREDNESS LIFESTYLE

My name is Ray Gano, and I have led some sort of preparedness lifestyle all my life. Even when I was growing up, I remember having a secret stash of food, my "James Bond" gear, and a camping knife that was about six inches long and had everything on it except the kitchen sink. I used to go into our backyard and make all sorts of funky traps to catch "bad guys," then make my parents come out and watch the traps in action. (Nine times out of ten, they didn't work.)

One night, when a friend and I were up watching late-night TV, we saw a recruiting commercial for the U.S. Army that said, "Come Join the Rangers." We were sick of working at the pizza joint, and were eager for some adventure in the elite, special operations force. So the next day, we both signed up for 11BP Infantry/Airborne. The recruiter told us that once we got to our permanent duty station, we could apply to go to Ranger.

He lied.

The nice thing, though, was that I was stationed at the best place: Fort Bragg, North Carolina, home of the 82nd Airborne/

Special Forces and Delta Force—even though Delta "never existed." In other words, it was so secretive that the U.S. government never acknowledged its existence. For those who do not know, Delta Force, along with its Navy counterpart, the SEALS, are the United States' primary counterterrorism units. So for "not existing," there were plenty of those Delta Force guys walking around Bragg. I loved the training at Bragg and the 82nd. We called it "High Drag, Low Speed, Ginzu Operated."

I have been through airborne school and advanced airborne (where we got to jump out of perfectly good helicopters). Survival, Escape, Evade, and Recon—also known as SEAR School—was pretty intense. After we trained for a week in survival skills, land navigation, etc., we were dropped by a C-130 aircraft on the opposite side of Fort Bragg with a map, a compass, a knife, and a ready-to-eat meal called a LERP (long-range patrol rations). If you take it slowly, you can stretch the LERP for almost two days.

We worked in pairs, and the goal was for my partner—a corporal—and me to get back to the barracks as fast as we could without being caught. If we were caught, we would be sent to prisoner-of-war camp, where we would become the property of Physiological Operations Warfare (Phy-Ops). The guys there are the professional interrogators who crawl into your mind and break you.

Did I have to go to Phy-Ops? No! Thankfully, my partner and I did not get caught. We played it smart, sleeping during the day and traveling at night, going out of our way to stay off the main roads and firebreaks. We took the long way, which extended the trip to four and a half days—but we made it.

While I was in the army, I had the opportunity to go through a lot of training the average infantry soldier does not receive. At that time, Special Operations was a part of the 82nd Airborne, which included Special Forces, Ranger Battalion, and 10th Mountain's light infantry—the latter having been newly introduced. We were all part of the rapid-response forces during the Ronald Reagan presidency.

I was assigned to B Co. 2/505, and our mission was to fight behind enemy lines in small squads and teams—disrupting enemy operations, pushing the enemy back, and holding that line until the regular army came. Once it arrived, we resupplied, put on our parachutes, boarded the plane, and did it all over again.

At that time, each of the battalions at 82nd had a special focus. Some specialized in desert warfare, others in mountain and forest areas. Ours focused on jungle operations. Because of this, we were sent to Panama to the JOTC (Jungle Operations Training Center), the U.S. Army's training center for light infantry and special operations units from 1953 to 1999.

The day we jumped in, we were told to wear an old pair of jungle BDUs (battle dress uniforms, or fatigues) and gloves. We did as we were told—and were glad of it, because the short drop zone was in elephant grass that was as tall as I am, and it was razor sharp, able to cut a uniform to shreds. Our survival skills were greatly honed and expanded down there: We learned how to eat monkeys, snakes, and just about anything else that crawled. We also got our fill of insects, spiders, coconut grubs, and grasshoppers. We learned to avoid certain trees such as the black palm, which has large, porcupine-like thorns sticking out all along the trunk. We also found food to enjoy, including delicious fruit such as mangos.

I look back on my days in the military with fondness and

sometimes even a bit of regret over not doing my twenty years. The experience built much of my preparedness and survival skills, but the real eye-opener for me was the Loma Prieta earthquake in 1998.

The Loma Prieta earthquake, also known as the Quake of '89 and the World Series Earthquake, struck the San Francisco Bay area of California at 5:04 PM local time on October 17, 1989. Caused by a slip along the San Andreas Fault, the tremor lasted ten to fifteen seconds and measured 6.9 on the Moment Magnitude scale. It had a surface-wave magnitude of 7.1. The quake killed sixty-three people throughout northern California; it injured 3,757 and left some three thousand to twelve thousand people homeless.[1]

I had an opportunity to work with FEMA (the Federal Emergency Management Agency) inspecting homes damaged in this disaster. From this experience, I observed a common regret—one expressed over and over by people who had lost everything: They wished they had put family pictures in a safe place. Those who found their pictures while digging through the rubble reacted as if they had struck gold. (This is why I now keep a stack of family pictures and other photos of importance in my BOB—my "Bug-Out Bag." That is my seventy-two hour kit containing enough supplies to last for three days in case of an emergency. It includes food, water, clothing, medical supplies, camping gear, sleeping gear, and other essential items.) Those raised in the San Francisco Bay area are bombarded with information about earthquake preparedness. They learn from an early age to get into a bathtub, under a desk, or next to something large during a quake so if the building falls down around them, they will have an air pocket for breathing. Many people have five-gallon-bucket sur-

SURVIVE THE COMING STORM

vival kits, which vary from really elaborate ones to ones containing little other than an AM/FM radio.

My family was no exception; we kept supplies—camping gear, tents, etc.—on hand and ready to go in case an earthquake should occur. In that event, we were instructed to head outside if possible, and we agreed on a place to meet if we were ever separated. I even had my special "James Bond" gear packed in a little backpack with my stash of food and other stuff.

With that preparedness lifestyle in my background, I've continued to try to learn how to live off the land, no matter where I am—even if it means learning how to survive in the city or urban environment.

As a family, we always had a huge garden full of produce; the extra, my mom always canned or dehydrated. Food was never wasted. We were one of the first families to get the heat-sealed bags, the forerunners of today's zip-topped or vacuum-sealed bags.

My parents never wasted an opportunity to catch food, so days at the beach meant we could go fishing and crabbing. Always, at the end of the day, the ice chest would be filled with plenty of fresh seafood ready to freeze. This type of resourcefulness is sorely lacking these days.

When I entered the eighth grade, my parents got me my first Crosman BB/pellet gun, which had just hit the market. It was the famous .766 Crosman, a great gun that is still manufactured today. I learned that, even in the city, one can find rabbits in the overflow ditches and creeks. What I shot, I brought home—and true to form, Mom would cook the game up for me.

Why have I been teaching, writing, and speaking about what I call proper Christian stewardship and preparedness? Because the next "big one" is still coming. By this, I mean a catastrophe is always around the corner, whether it's the next earthquake, flood, or hurricane.

Although this book is about preparedness, the focus is on what I believe will be manmade things to come that can severely affect us if we are not prepared. One of the major issues I've been keeping an eye on is the financial tailspin our nation and the world are taking.

For the past five years, I have not only tried to warn others about this financial crisis or "coming storm," but I've also tried to pass on, to those who will open their eyes and pay attention, the survival skills gleaned over my lifetime.

Many other things, which I will discuss later, threaten this nation as well, but I believe we are closer to financial disaster than we are to being nuked, EMP (electromagnetic pulse)[2] attacked, or becoming the victims of another 9/11/01-type of event that would rock this nation. In the age of digital money and financial transactions taking place at the speed of light, the demise of this country can happen in a matter of days, if not hours.

Let me say that I don't believe that what Hollywood has portrayed through films like *Mad Max* and *I Am Legend* offer an accurate picture of things to come. Films and books like those may have great plot lines, but they are not realistic. Many lessons from modern-day history demonstrate that life goes on after a crisis, but it is drastically changed for the worse.

It is not a matter of IF a financial disaster will take place; it is a matter of WHEN. And when it does, we just might wake up one morning with the television news announcers stating that all the banks across the nation have been closed by the government. This official "bank holiday" will make it impossible for customers to get to their money. Credit cards will no longer work, and no one will be accepting checks. The economy will be operating on a "cash-on-demand" system—or, if you were one of those who thought ahead, you might have some sort of tangible assets that can be traded for goods, services, or even cash itself.

Can you imagine the chaos, riots, and turmoil that will take place because of an economic catastrophe such as this? Remember the Los Angeles riots of 1992? Also known as the "Rodney King Uprising," this incident was sparked by disagreement with the "not-guilty" verdict for the police who viciously beat Rodney King during a traffic stop. For six days following that decision, people rioted, looted stores, homes, and restaurants, and set fire to a large portion of south-central Los Angeles. More than fifty-five people were killed, and two thousand-plus were injured. It is estimated that over $8 million (and some put that figure closer to $1 billion) of damage was done. Multiply that by 300–500 percent, and place a similar riot in every major city across the nation. Remember that even while all of this is occurring, people will still go to work, children will attend school, and somehow life will move on.

We will have to contend with a major rise in crime, a lack of money, a shortage of food, and a good chance that everything around us will break down due to there being no upkeep. The tough times will cause most people to stop caring. Public services will erode drastically, public welfare programs will stop functioning, and public hospitals and medical facilities will become severely overburdened. Just going to the grocery store will require detailed logistics, dependable security, and the right type of weaponry.

These are just some of the events that have already taken place in countries like Zimbabwe, Bolivia, and Argentina. In fact, prior to 2001, Argentina was not the "banana republic" it is viewed as being today. It was actually a richer, more thriving country than the United States was back in the 1980s. Many Argentineans took weekend shopping trips to New York City or visited Orlando's Disney World. But even these activities were passé to the very wealthy of Argentina, who would take shopping trips to the Mediterranean, hopping from one Greek island to the next, or spend the day in Paris or the French Riviera.

What happened there could very likely take place in the United States.

Can you imagine paying $32 billion (U.S. dollars) for a dozen eggs? That is exactly what eggs are going for in Zimbabwe today, where hyperinflation has a dragon's grip on the nation—with no escape in sight. The country just keeps printing more money and raising the denomination of its currency. A few years ago, the currency was thousand Z-dollars; later, million Z-dollar bills were being printed; and today, the 100-billion Z-dollar bill is being printed and placed into circulation.

The Goal of This Book

During devastating global events and worldwide catastrophes, the population will include three types of people: sheep, wolves, and sheepdogs. It is my goal to help you become the sheepdog who will protect your family, loved ones, and neighbors by knowing how to survive, how to provide for those who will depend on you, and—I hope—how to maintain a good quality of life filled with the love and help of our loving Heavenly Father. Another part of my goal is to make sure that those of us who follow Christ will be in a position to help others, thus opening a door to share the gospel.

About 80 percent of the people in the world today have no clue about what is coming. The overriding concern of all too many is a narrow focus on trivial things like Monday night football—and on having enough pizza and beer to go along with it. They honestly think that life is grand, our country is prosperous, and we will remain that way for as long as this nation is called the United States of America.

But what is going to happen when, all of a sudden, this "mob" wakes up and realizes that their world filled with football, beer, and pizza no longer exists? What will the shelves at the local mega mart look like?

Did you know that this nation only maintains a three-day supply of goods on its store shelves—and that is on a good day? Merchandise is trucked in every night, the shelves are restocked, and what seems like a "magic place" keeps the food, goods, and other items on hand so that we can come in and get what we need and want, pretty much any time our hearts desire.

What will the gas prices at the local gas station look like? Remember the 1970s gas lines wrapping around city blocks? People were getting up at four o'clock in the morning on the specified days—odd or even—in the hopes that they would be able to purchase gas. Do you perhaps remember being one of those who was turned away because the station ran out of gas? Can you imagine what it would be like if the local gas station did not get any gas for a week or longer? Would tempers flare? How would you get to work? We need to realize that even during crisis, the world will continue. The wheels and cogs of business will keep moving forward. History has proven time and again that people adapt and overcome. Those who do not prepare or have the means to weather the storms will be left behind to suffer with what little charity can be found, which will quickly diminish and will most likely perish.

If you want another reminder of what might happen, read up on the Great Depression. How many families' lives were ruined? How many people died because they didn't look ahead? I know I am painting a bleak picture of doom and gloom, but I describe these pictures to illustrate the fact that there is hope. But you need to do something now, while there is still time to prepare. The prophet Daniel read the handwriting on the wall and warned King Nebuchadnezzar about how quickly his kingdom would be taken from him. Joseph acted on the information of knowing seven lean years were to come by using the seven years of prosperity he was given to build and fill the granaries. He became a blessing not only to his own family, but to the nations around him.

Scripture says:

- "Go to the ant, thou sluggard; consider her ways, and be wise" (Proverbs 6:6).
- "How long wilt thou sleep, O sluggard? when wilt thou arise out of thy sleep?" (Proverbs 6:9).
- "The ants are a people not strong, yet they prepare their meat in the summer" (Proverbs 30:25).

Most people haven't been paying attention. You may have been one of these people, but what makes you different now is that you are waking up from your stupor, and the sheepdog within you is starting to emerge. You are finding that you do care about tomorrow, and that you want to provide for your family—especially in the hard times to come.

If you are a Bible-believing Christian, you may have felt this urge for a while, but you may have had no idea of what to do about it. Most pastors are not discussing what is really going on. Many are more worried about the new church building fund or some church activity within the community. In fact, it seems that pastors are mostly concerned with keeping everyone happy— keeping happy fannies in the pews and making sure the offering plates continue to go around and around.

You may not be learning about things to come in Sunday school, and when you ask others about what to expect, you may be given some sugar-coated answer accusing you of not trusting God to provide. Or, you may get a look as if you are some strange person looking for little green men and black helicopters. In fact, it seems like many out there have forgotten why we are here on this third rock from the sun.

Scripture says: "But sanctify the Lord God in your hearts: and be ready always to give an answer to every man that asketh you a reason of the hope that is in you, with meekness and fear" (1 Peter 3:15).

It also states: "Go ye therefore, and teach all nations, baptizing them in the name of the Father, and of the Son, and of the Holy Ghost: Teaching them to observe all things whatsoever I have commanded you: and, lo, I am with you alway, even unto the end of the world. Amen" (Matthew 28:19–20).

Many people have forgotten the Great Commission. They have either focused on things that really do not matter, or they have their heads buried in the sand, ignoring all that is going on around them. They have given up—so much so that the very souls of their loved ones who do not know Him no longer matter. They have forgotten what they could do for the Lord and His Kingdom.

But how did we get here?

Part I

chapter one

THE COMING STORM
How Did We Get Here?

One day I was in the car listening to a local talk radio program that piqued my interest. The topic centered on finance, oil, the future, etc., and presented the typical corporate/financial spiel. Someone listening to the program who didn't know how the corporate financial world worked would have really been impressed: The featured guest had a string of titles and letters behind his name, as well as "years of experience," but I wasn't impressed. In fact, I was kind of upset because he was selling the audience down the river. What was he selling? The typical finance mantra: "Work hard, save money, get out of debt, invest for the long term, and diversify, diversify, diversify."

Warren Buffett, one of the world's greatest investors, said, "Diversification is a protection against ignorance. It makes very little sense for those who know what they are doing." The corporate financial mantra is for those who don't know what they are doing. I was in the finance arena long enough to know that it was not what it was cracked up to be. That mantra was my mantra. It was mine because that was what I was told to say by all the higher-ups—after all, it was my job. It was a serious struggle to sell a worldly plan based on mammon (money), which I knew had serious faults. Many of these faults are based on fear and a lack of financial education on the part of the buyer.

Because I am a Bible-believing Christian, I also had the advantage of knowing what God's Word says. The Word of God is sovereign, and it tells me a different story about where the future is going. It is *not* going where all the so-called financial experts hawking products that feed the corrupt financial services system say it's headed. In fact, many of those people are realizing that as well. (That's why I got out of that field. I was sick of being told to lie to people I truly cared about.)

What upset me, also, was that the host of the radio show really didn't seem to know any better, either. He went right along with his guest, and even allowed a ten-minute, subtle infomercial at the conclusion of the interview. The "expert" promoted his books, pushed his seminars, and even expressed a willingness to speak at local businesses or churches—free. Now that is a great deal! Or is it?

What the host of the program did not know was that his guest was going to sell everyone he met down the river, as I stated before. And guess what? The clients would walk away feeling great about the whole experience because they would not even know that they had just bought into a bunch of garbage and possible financial slavery.

A History Lesson and the Road Ahead

As you may understand well by now, I do not have much faith in the U.S. economy maintaining its stability. In fact, being a student of Bible prophecy, I do not have *any* faith in any economy maintaining stability in these last days, because God's Word says that it won't.

Some readers may remember the 1970s, when many very interesting events took place that are now affecting our nation and the world. Where we are today is due to the decisions made way back then.

In the 1970s, OPEC (Organization of Petroleum Exporting Companies) and the United States created what is called the petrodollar. This provided the U.S. with a virtual monopoly. Oil being traded in U.S. dollars allowed America to run huge account deficits.

Here is how it worked: Countries needed oil; thus, they had to have U.S. dollars on hand so they could purchase that oil. The U.S. dollar became the standard of what is called the global currency reserve. It allowed the nation to spend without the fear of crippling interest-rate hikes. And spend we have, to the point of self destruction and the creation of a fiat currency.

Fiat Currency

In economics, fiat currency or fiat money is money that derives its purchasing power from a declaration by the government issuing the currency. It is often associated with paper money that isn't backed by fixed assets, issued without the promise of redemption in some other form, and accepted by tradition or social convention. Fiat money is called "fiduciary money" in many languages.

The widespread acceptance of a fiat currency is enhanced by a central authority mandating its acceptance under penalty of law and demanding it in payment of taxes or tribute. Fiat money can be contrasted with alternative forms of currency, such as commodity money and private currency.

Most currencies in the world have been fiat money since the end of the international gold standard of the Bretton Woods system in 1971. However, some of the major currencies today, despite being based essentially on arbitrary decree, have become so trusted that they are termed "hard currency."[3]

> If the American people ever allow private banks to control the issue of their money, first by inflation and then by deflation, the banks and corporations that will grow up around them will deprive the people of their property until their children will wake up homeless on the continent their fathers conquered.

This quote has often been erroneously attributed to Thomas Jefferson. Regardless of their source, the words capture a thought that we know to be consistent with the third president's viewpoint. Jefferson fought—and warned about—the creation of the Federal Reserve or any private bank that would control the United States' money. He was well aware of the subject, because in his day the international bankers were trying to establish a central bank or Federal Reserve.

Blake's Dictionary of Law defines "fiat" as follows: "A command or order to act. Arbitrary or authoritative order or decision." "Fiat money" is likewise defined as: "Inconvertible paper money made legal tender by a government decree" (inconvertible to, for example, gold or silver). "Colored money" is defined as money with the "deceptive appearance, assumed exterior, concealing a lack of reality."[4]

The money we use today is called Federal Reserve Notes, and it is *colored money*. If you do not believe me, whip out a twenty-dollar bill and check it out for yourself. In fact, look at the really new money out there now; it is a lot less green than the money in circulation during days gone by. The bills have no value, except by virtue of a government decree. Here is another interesting point: All fiat currencies eventually go belly up—and with them, the countries that produce them.

But quickly back to OPEC and the petrodollar.

Bill O'Grady of A. G. Edwards financial services company stated, "If OPEC decided they didn't want dollars anymore, it would be the end of American hegemony by signaling the end to the dollar as the sole reserve currency."[5] So why do we need to know all this history?

In 1971, President Richard Nixon changed the rules of money. That year, the U.S. dollar ceased being money and became a currency. This was one of the most important changes in modern history, but few people understand why.

Before 1971, the U.S. dollar had been backed by gold and silver, which is why it was also known as a silver certificate. After 1971, the U.S. dollar became a Federal Reserve Note—basically, an IOU from the U.S. government. Needless to say, the U.S. has so many IOUs out there that the reality of paying them back is next to impossible. The U.S. is now the largest debtor nation in history.

We need to understand this, because history always repeats itself.

After World War I, Germany's monetary system collapsed. While there were many reasons for this, one major factor was that the German government was allowed to print money at will, like we are currently doing. The flood of money that resulted caused uncontrolled inflation, which is starting to take place right now. The more Germany printed marks, the less merchandise the citizens bought. In 1913, a pair of shoes cost thirteen marks. By 1923, that same pair of shoes was 32 trillion marks! As inflation increased, the savings of the middle class was wiped out. With its savings gone, the middle class demanded new leadership. Adolf Hitler was elected chancellor of Germany in 1933, and, as we know, World War II and the murder of millions of Jews followed. This same pattern as mentioned above is beginning to be repeated right now in these United States of America.

That was the first part of our history lesson. Now, continuing to the second part...

In the 1970s, a law touted as a great one, a "law for the people," was created. Called ERISA, which stood for the Employee Retirement Income Security Act, this is the law that gave birth to the 401(k) tax-deferred savings program. One reason ERISA is significant is that it forced millions of employees to become investors—without any financial training or education. This is why the financial experts' advice is to "work hard, save money, get out of debt, invest for the long term, and diversify, diversify, diversify."

Warren Buffet made a great statement that sums up this strategy: "Wall Street is the only place that people ride to in a Rolls Royce to get advice from those that take the subway."[6]

Many people know that the baby boomer generation is the largest in history. Many companies have made millions from this population explosion. When the baby boomers had babies,

Gerber baby food made millions. When the baby boomer babies got older, Mattel, Hasbro, and other toy companies made millions. Because the baby boomers grew up to live life at high speed, fast-food places like McDonald's and Burger King were born. I point these things out because the baby boomers are a generation to be considered. When they buy products or services, companies make millions.

Baby boomers have money saved for retirement via their 401(k)s, IRAs, etc. Between 1995 and 2005, the millions of people who followed the "work hard, save money, get out of debt, invest for the long term, and diversify, diversify, diversify" advice lost an estimated $7–9 trillion. And much worse than losing $7–9 trillion, the people who followed that advice missed out on what *The Economist* and other magazines called the biggest financial boom in history. So, not only did those investors lose money from the 2000–2003 stock market crash, but they failed to make a lot of money in the financial boom in real estate and commodities. That is the price of bad advice, and even worse is not having the knowledge/education to know differently.

But back to ERISA…

ERISA has a major flaw that many people do not look at or even know about. *It has a mandatory withdrawal mechanism at age seventy and a half.* At that age, you MUST start withdrawing your money from the 401(k)s, IRAs, etc. That means millions of baby boomers will be forced to withdraw their retirement savings.

Where is all this money reinvested? You guessed it—in the stock market. As I stated before, when the baby boomers BOUGHT, companies made millions. In 2006, the first baby boomers turned sixty. What will happen when the baby boomers start to sell?

In 2016, it is estimated that there will be 2,282,887 baby boomers turning seventy. They all must start selling and pulling their money out of the stock market. In 2017, that number jumps to 2,928,818 people. That is about seven hundred thousand more people than the year before who will start selling and pulling their money out of the stock market, too.[7]

That is 5,211,705 people altogether! That many people will affect the economy dramatically—and more are added each year for approximately twenty years. (Please note that immigrants are not counted in this figure.)[8]

All in all, that is a lot of stock being sold, or at least trying to be sold.

What happens when millions of people start selling millions of shares of stock? The prices start to drop, and fast. The laws of supply and demand will come into effect, and the odds of a major panic occurring will increase enormously.

So, why is there a mandatory withdrawal? Why not just change the law? All the money that was put into the market was put there tax free. Uncle Sam now wants his due…the taxes. This is another reason for the huge spending, the fiat currency, etc. This is also why we will probably never see the death tax go away any time soon.

Knowing this, how many countries are going to keep buying dollars? Wouldn't it be wiser to start finding another secure global currency reserve prior to this happening? What about possibly making their own currencies a global currency reserve?

That is part two of our history lesson. Now, let's fast forward to today and look at where we are.

Social Security is officially doling out more than it is taking in. That was not supposed to take place until 2013–2014. Social Security announced that in March, 2010.[9]

We have seen a major crash in the housing industry. The price of gold is maintaining over thirteen hundred dollars an ounce, and silver is sitting around forty dollars an ounce. All the while, the dollar is losing more ground daily.

There is speculation that the next bubble to burst will be the credit bubble. This will affect everyone who has a credit card or extended credit with banks and other lending organizations. This bubble popping will drastically affect the flow of money.

The current administration has spent more money than all the past administrations put together.[10]

We no longer need those silly things called printing presses to print more money. All we do now, in this digital age, is go to the magic computer screen and type out more ZEROS. Millions, billions, trillions…who cares? It is just zeros.

Our Immediate Future

At the end of July 2010, annualized growth had slowed to 2.4 percent. The gross domestic product (GDP) was down for a second quarter. But the money changers knew that was coming. They saw it in December 2009 when those numbers were released. In fact, even Ben Bernanke, the Federal Reserve chairman, described the economy as "unusually uncertain" in terms of its outlook.

What we are seeing as of this writing is what is called "contracting" money. In other words, the money supply is getting bloated, but cash flow is slowing. People are holding on to their cash. Banks are refusing to loan, even when they have millions and billions in assets. More money gets pumped into the system, but like a balloon, it just expands…going nowhere.

Our nation has been experiencing this "bloating" for several years; some analysts point as far back as 2007. When money contracts year after year, it is a major signal for a downturn. Not only that, but many of the financial pundits are saying we need to brace for an intensified downturn.

How does this happen?

When cash flow is "squeezed" and liquidity becomes an issue, business activity slows. It becomes a vicious circle, much like a vortex in the ocean. People are not spending money out of fear. Because of that, business activity slows and employees get furloughed or even laid off; as a result, they have no money to spend. Do you see how this cycle almost propels itself? The result is an ever-growing depression, and it is taking place today.

The media will describe it as a "double-dip" recession, but the nation has never really had a full-blown recovery. We have used some form of stimulus money to "spend" ourselves out of trouble. The problem with that, though, is that our government has been borrowing the money to keep our economy alive, worsening the effects of a depression. This is the same thing that Herbert Hoover and Franklin D. Roosevelt did during the Great Depression.

But we never had a recovery.

Imagine a ski slope with a very deep downturn—down, down, down. All of a sudden, stimulus money is thrown at the problem and we get an upturn, or a ski jump, of sorts. We are the skier, picking up speed down the slopes of the economy. We have hit the ski jump created by the stimulus, and now we are sailing through the air. We feel great and exhilarated. But...all of a sudden, we look down and see what is happening. We realize that the laws of cause and effect are coming into play. We start spinning wildly in the air as we try to figure out which end is up. We then take a pretty bad tumble.

So where are we now? We have left the ski jump, we have realized where we are, and we have begun to spin in the air. How many of you have remembered to put on your parachute? You need one so that when you do hit that bump and go flying off into the air like everyone else, you have a way to soften the fall.

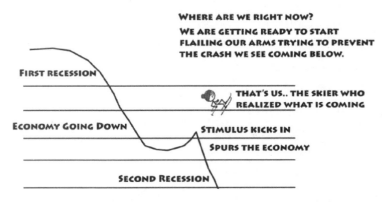

WHERE ARE WE RIGHT NOW?
WE ARE GETTING READY TO START FLAILING OUR ARMS TRYING TO PREVENT THE CRASH WE SEE COMING BELOW.

FIRST RECESSION

THAT'S US.. THE SKIER WHO REALIZED WHAT IS COMING

ECONOMY GOING DOWN

STIMULUS KICKS IN

SPURS THE ECONOMY

SECOND RECESSION

Remember, Noah built an ark to prepare for the rain (God did not build the ark for him). Joseph spent seven plentiful years storing up food for seven years of famine. These men had "parachutes" for their protection during the coming emergencies. They listened to the warnings from God and took action. They experienced falls, but their landings were safe because they had put on their "preparedness parachutes." They did what they knew they should do and left the rest up to God. Notice in each of those stories that preparation took years; readiness for the coming crisis did not happen overnight. However, anything you can do now will take you one step closer to being able to safely endure the event.

The issue of stewardship has been on my mind for quite some time, and I can't hold back my voice or my efforts anymore. We are living in the last days, and we know the outcome. The sad thing is that many have forgotten why we are here.

In fact, something horrible has happened here in this nation, and it is showing up all over the world. People generally believe that just because we are the greatest country in the world and just because God loves this nation so much, He will not allow us to go through hard times or persecution. In other words, many out there believe that God's throne is draped in the good old "red, white, and blue." The real sad thing is that so many have used this as an excuse for inaction instead of as an impetus for action.

Why? Because many have used the Rapture as an excuse to do nothing instead of allowing it to spur one to action. It is like these people have rolled over and said, "Who cares? Let's eat, drink, and be merry, because the Rapture is coming and we have nothing to worry about." Those who have this attitude have forgotten the Great Commission and the greatest commandment. They have chosen things that really don't matter rather than the very souls of the loved ones they could affect for the Lord. It seems like so many people have been lulled into some sort of sluggard's stupor, like the proverbial deer in the headlights that doesn't know what to do.

The Boy Scouts' motto is "Be Prepared." "Be Prepared" for what? "Be Prepared" for anything! Live a life of anticipation as well as urgency. Scripture tells us to always be ready: "But sanctify the Lord God in your hearts: and be ready always to give an answer to every man that asketh you a reason of the hope that is in you with meekness and fear" (1 Peter 3:15).

We need to "be ready always" to share the gospel in good times and in bad. We Christians must not lose the fight within us. We need to fight for tomorrow, fight for that loved one across town, fight for that coworker. We have to shake off complacency, stand up, and fight.

Now, you may stand on two familiar passages in the book of Matthew:

Matthew 6:25: "Therefore I say unto you, Take no thought for your life, what ye shall eat, or what ye shall drink; nor yet for your body, what ye shall put on. Is not the life more than meat, and the body than raiment?"

Matthew 6:31: "Therefore take no thought, saying, What shall we eat? or, What shall we drink? or, Wherewithal shall we be clothed?"

Using these verses as an excuse for laziness, however, is taking Scripture out of context. Many people make God out to be the "great welfare agent in the sky," a type of "sugar daddy." He is neither.

God provides for all of our needs. But He sure doesn't plant twenty-dollar-bill trees in the backyard. I haven't witnessed pennies falling from heaven, have you? God provides His blessings by setting opportunities before us. When we are being diligent for Him through the work we do for the Kingdom, He will provide for all our needs. We need to work, prepare, and always be ready:

"For even when we were with you, this we commanded you, that if any would not work, neither should he eat" (2 Thessalonians 3:10).

"Go to the ant, thou sluggard; consider her ways, and be wise" (Proverbs 6:6).

Leaning upon Matthew 6:25 and 6:31 as an excuse for inactivity has turned many people into sluggards. But God does not contradict His Word: "But if any provide not for his own, and especially for those of his own house, he hath denied the faith, and is worse than an infidel" (1 Timothy 5:8).

A Word to Men

Now, I want to speak specifically to male readers for a moment. Please read the following and ask yourself, "What am I doing about it?"

It really gets my goat when I hear some folks say that I am some radical, survivalist, gun-toting nut for having the concern to make sure that my family is taken care of. I often hear, "Ray, you just don't trust God to provide—and besides, look around you. The Rapture is coming any day now."

Many people have home insurance, car insurance, life insurance, health insurance, renter's insurance, and so forth. How many people are willing to give those up because the Rapture could take place within the next few days? Is it wrong to put food "insurance" in place?

"Where is your faith now?" I ask the people who have home, car, life, and health insurance. Don't they trust God? Why do they have all these things in place if they are quoting Matthew 6:31?

In fact, if they quote Matthew 6:31, then why shouldn't they also do as instructed in Luke 18:22—"Sell all that thou hast, and distribute unto the poor, and thou shalt have treasure in heaven: and come, follow me"? It seems like hypocrisy. What guarantee can anyone give that we will NOT be here this time next year? What about three, five, or ten years from now?

I know that I am pushing the limits with many people; in

fact, some may be saying, "Ray has gone off the deep end. He is turning into one of those...you know...Post-Tribbers."

As I have said, I stand firmly upon the Lord's imminent return. In fact, this very doctrine of imminence is what fuels the fire that I have burning within, compelling me to say these things. I see great opportunities. I look out at the sea of people, including myself, and ask, "Have I really given my all, or am I merely paying lip service? Do I really believe that He is coming soon, or am I just playing that church game that many of us play?"

Very hard times are coming to this nation. That is a hardcore, 100-percent fact. The problem is that about 80 percent of us don't care and 20 percent of us are getting somewhat involved in the game. And of the 20 percent, 10 percent of us are on the field of battle, and 2 percent are fighting the fight.

It all boils down to the fact that we have forgotten to "occupy till He returns" (see Luke 19:13). No one can guarantee that we are not going to be here this time next year. Only God knows the timeline for end-times events. So we need to wake up to this reality, put on our armor, and fight the good fight instead of being the yellow-bellied cowards many of us have been for the past twenty to thirty years.

It is time to plant the standard of God and say to the enemy, "NO MORE!!!" With this stated, we need to ground ourselves and look at what tomorrow really brings. It isn't going to be coming up roses; the weeds of tough times are ahead.

chapter two

CRISIS MELTDOWN

Crisis Deepens; Chaos Grips Greece
Greece Protests: Riots Erupt in Athens,
Three Bank Workers Killed

ATHENS—Greece's fiscal crisis took a new turn to violence Wednesday when three people died in a firebomb attack amid a paralyzing national strike, while governments from Spain to the U.S. took steps to prevent the widening financial damage from hitting their own economies.

In Spain, rival political leaders came together Wednesday with an agreement that aims to shore up shaky savings banks by the end of next month. Banks in France and Germany, which are among Greece's top creditors, pledged to support a Greek bailout by continuing to lend to the country. Investors, meanwhile, are pouring money into bonds of countries seen as less exposed to the crisis, from Russia to Egypt.

Anxiety over the Euro-zone economies sent the Euro down to about 1.29 to the dollar, its lowest level in more than a year. The Dow Jones Industrial Average fell for the second straight day, losing 58.65 points, or 0.54 percent, to close at 10868.12.[11]

If you have not been paying attention to what is going on in Greece, you need to, because this foreshadows things to come here in the United States. People in today's society have bought into the Hollywood scenario of the apocalyptic worlds of *Mad Max* and *Mad Max Beyond Thunder Dome*. When crisis hits, we are not going to resort to being Will Smith's character in the *I Am Legend* world. Life will go on as soon as the main crisis slows down. It will just be a completely different world than the one we used to live in. Those who have prepared will successfully make the transition; those who haven't will fall by the wayside and become casualties of the crisis.

Everyone is worried about EMP, or a nuke attack and zombies. Can these things happen? Sure…well, maybe not the zombies…but the odds are pretty high of these things not happening at all. (However, there may be a bunch of zombies walking around in a daze at the sudden change in the status of their financial security.) As I've often stated, the odds of a financial crisis hitting this country are very good. In fact, I am going to say again that it isn't a matter of "IF," it is a matter of "WHEN."

One of the greatest teachers is history itself, and it is a teacher we often ignore. Yet consider what the Word of God says: "The thing that hath been, it is that which shall be; and that which is done is that which shall be done: and there is no new thing under the sun" (Ecclesiastes 1:9).

What we are seeing in Greece is a repeat of history. This is the same thing that took place in Bolivia, Zimbabwe, and Argentina just in the last decade. A financial crisis is here; the masses just don't know it yet. It isn't zombies we will be fighting; our fight will be against the crime, high prices, sporadic water services, and frequently interrupted electric service. Out of all these changes, it is the crime that will sooner or later be like nothing we've ever seen. Again, history and the sin nature of man will show this to be true.

When catastrophe strikes, you'll feel a real urgent need to increase your security habits and try to find means of self defense. The problem is that the million or so other people who live in your general area will have the same urgent need.

Want to get a gun? Sorry, the shelves will be empty—or they will cost so much that it will be virtually impossible. Those who are prepared will have already taken their personal, family, and home security needs into consideration. This is why I highly encourage you to get a carry-and-conceal license *now*. On top of that, take at least some basic classes on how to handle the weapon and even on some close-quarter combat tactics. Classes are out there; local gun shop owners can usually provide that information.

What about some sort of home alarm system, security system, or even automatic lights? After a catastrophe, the prices of these systems will go through the roof. Not only will money be basically worthless, but there will be competition among millions of consumers who are looking for the same things. Those who are prepared will have already set up these types of systems as well. Being prepared affords the freedom and peace of mind to make sound decisions to help family, friends, and neighbors, who no doubt will be calling upon you for help. When the economy crashes or some other type of disaster hits, you will not be able to afford to make ignorant mistakes. Mistakes can cost you money and, God forbid, possibly your life.

As mentioned earlier, people will naturally be divided into three groups: the "sheepdogs," the "sheep," and the "wolves." It is the wolves with whom the sheep and the sheepdogs will need to contend.

What about a Job and Food?

Just as during the Great Depression, the days, weeks, and months following a calamitous economic crisis will find people job hunting for extended periods of time—possibly for years. Competing for a job will become an art form of its own. Monster job-search websites and the classified ads will be a joke, because in the "New Normal" that will have been established, finding and securing a job will be more a matter of "who you know" than "what you know." Those who are prepared will have contacted friends of friends, established networks, and advertised their abilities to help them secure much-coveted jobs. And, as stated earlier, just getting to and from work will be an exercise in logistics, tactics, and determination. It will take nerves of steel to contend with the riots, road blocks, fires, car jackings, kidnappings, shootings, and looting occurring throughout many regions (and that's just to name a few of the potential obstacles).

Getting into grocery stores to purchase the limited food and supplies in stock will be like walking through the gauntlet. Customers must be "on alert" to get to and from their cars, using pepper spray or other means to keep the wolves at bay. Once inside, shoppers will have to contend with prices being 200–300 percent, possibly even 700 percent, higher than they are now, and paper money may be virtually worthless.

Once banks reopen after their government-imposed "holiday," they will limit withdrawal amounts. That's how it is now with the Reserve Bank of Zimbabwe (the equivalent to our own Federal Reserve), which has fixed the daily withdrawal limit at Z$100 billion. That is roughly $1.25 in U.S. currency per day for individuals, and doesn't even cover the average, day-to-day cost of living. The people of Zimbabwe are living in the country with the highest inflation rate in the world today. Prices are all fixed by the government. If they weren't, the cost would be astronomical. The shops that are open charge, on average, a 15-percent fee just for using Z-dollars because the hyperinflation is so rapid that within twenty-four hours, the merchants will have lost money due to rising prices.

Those who are prepared will have protected their wealth by putting it into silver, gold, jewelry, and other such assets. They may even have other hard currencies on hand like the Swiss francs, Chinese yuan, or other currencies that have not lost value in the world economy. These assets and solid currencies will purchase food, gas, and other day-to-day expenses—regardless of bank limits.

Now is the time to decide whether or not you will be prepared. Take this opportunity to prepare for this situation—now. Remember, history repeats itself. Life will go on after a major catastrophe, but it will be the end of the world as we know it; it will be a world with new rules and new attitudes.

Those who have prepared will have the upper hand and be able to transition. They will have already seen the writing on the wall for some time now. These people will be the sheepdogs.

What have the sheepdogs been doing all this time? That is coming later. What we need to focus on now are the coming storms. If we do not have a grasp on those, we will not know how to prepare—or even what to prepare for.

Other Storms on the Horizon

"My people are destroyed [perish] for lack of knowledge."
Hosea 4:6a

As stated previously, we need to be living as if the next minute were our last, as well as if we will be here for the next twenty or more years. This world is on the cusp of change, and how we prepare for that change is what will make a difference to us, our families, and those we care about. Remember, our goal is to make sure that our families and loved ones are cared for during a crisis so that we can be in the position to help even others outside of our circle, thus opening a door to share the gospel.

I believe the primary incident we need to prepare for is the demise and death of the United States' financial system. It is likely that we will see a massive deflationary movement, then a knee-jerk reaction to the situation in the form of printing huge amounts of money, thus causing massive hyperinflation. This major financial upheaval will wipe out most Americans' remaining savings, 401(k)s, IRAs, and other retirement savings accounts. In other words, the dollar will die. The primary "blast" will take place overnight, but how the government and banking organizations will deal with that crisis will cause the shock to stretch out for years.

Although financial calamity is, to me, the most likely scenario on the horizon, any number of events could occur to bring our lives into a state of crisis. But there are other storms we need to be aware of, and I hope to shine a little bit of light on several of the possibilities:

1. **Famine and other commodities shortages.** Already, the daily cost of food is rising. The cost of food worldwide has risen 37 percent from February 2010 to April 2011. Consecutive months have shown a continued increase.

2. **The rise of disease, illness, and pandemics.** With the dollar's demise, we lose the sanitation aspects of a first-world country and move to those of a third-world country, where germs and once-eradicated diseases will make a comeback.

3. **The global rise of Islam and the threat of a nuclear Iran.** This will give rise to…

4. **Terrorism, coupled with dirty bombs and possibly a nuclear detonation on U.S. or European soil.** This will be a direct result of the weakened state of the West triggered by the financial ruin.

5. **Marxist socialism, more aggressive regulations, and enhanced government control over the private sector.** This will stifle the small businesses and further slow the money flow.

6. **The "blame game," which will start globally and prompt global rejection of Israel.** I believe that Genesis 12:3—"And I will bless them that bless thee, and curse him that curseth thee: and in thee

shall all families of the earth be blessed"—will come into effect with the result of more natural disasters and "acts of God" for the rejection of His people and His land, Israel.

7. **The rejection and criminalization of Christianity.** Part of the blame game will be directed at Christians. It is our "laws" and capitalistic ways that created the global situation we are in. We will be called "hate mongers" and "intolerant" of others, resulting in the possible need for us to go into hiding.

8. **The rise of a luciferian religion, in which many of the world's religions will join forces under one banner.** Out of this religion, the one known as the Antichrist will emerge.

Now I want to clarify here that this scenario I'm describing may sound like the Tribulation spoken of by John in the book of Revelation. Just let me say this: What I am describing is a cake walk compared to what will take place during the Tribulation.

Part II

PREPARING FOR THE STORM

Food, Water, Gear, and Gadgets

chapter three

SHEEP, WOLVES, AND SHEEPDOGS

I have already mentioned the three categories of people every-one will fall into: sheep, wolves, and sheepdogs. This is a famous analogy that Lt. Col. Dave Grossman wrote about in his popular paper entitled *On Sheep, Wolves, and Sheepdogs,* in which he cat-egorizes people as follows.

The Sheep

These people are doing nothing about the coming storm. They think that tomorrow will be OK; they assume that the govern-ment will take care of them; and they believe that everything will always be rosy.

What happens to sheep is that they are led to be slaughtered of their own accord. In other words, they allow it to happen of their own free will, offering no resistance.

Why? Because they don't know what else to do. They have been indoctrinated to always follow orders, to do as they are told, to respect authority, to get in line, to wait patiently, and to "push 1 for English."

When the coming storm hits, this group of people will be devastated. They will be the ones standing in the soup kitchen lines, waiting on welfare, and asking for handouts because they will have done nothing to prepare for the future…even when they saw it coming.

Partially, it will be their fault, primarily because they will not have paid attention to their surroundings and noticed the subtle changes taking place in the world today. They really do not care about Fox News, CNN, or what is going on in the world. Things like current events burden their minds, and they have a hard time making heads or tails of what is going on. So, they will find it easier to ignore their surroundings and just go on doing what they have been doing rather than giving any serious thought at all to the warning signs.

There's something that needs to always be remembered: The sheep are always the fodder to the wolf.

Scripture says:

- "Go to the ant, thou sluggard; consider her ways, and be wise" (Proverbs 6:6).
- "For even when we were with you, this we commanded you, that if any would not work, neither should he eat" (2 Thessalonians 3:10).
- "The ants are a people not strong, yet they prepare their meat in the summer" (Proverbs 30:25).

Consider recent news reports.

New Braunfels Police Make Arrest in Violent Stabbing

NEW BRAUNFELS, Texas—A forty-six-year-old man has been arrested in connection with a violent stabbing at a New Braunfels Wal-Mart. Police have charged Juan Leandro Villareal with aggravated robbery, a first-degree felony. New Braunfels police said Villareal stabbed a sixty-four-year-old woman several times at the store's parking lot around 11 AM Sunday.[12]

Layoffs to Gut East St. Louis Police Force

EAST ST. LOUIS—The Rev. Joseph Tracy said he's tired of going to funerals. And now, he suspects he'll be going to more of them.

"It's open field day now," said Tracy, the pastor of Straightway Baptist Church here. "The criminals are going to run wild."

Gang activity. Drug dealing. Cold-blooded killing. Tracy worries that a decision to shrink the police force by almost 30 percent will bring more of everything.

The pastor voiced his concern on Friday at a raucous special City Council meeting at which East St. Louis Mayor Alvin Parks announced that the city will lay off thirty-seven employees, including nineteen of its sixty-two police officers, eleven firefighters, four public works employees, and three administrators. The layoffs take effect on Sunday.[13]

It is already a zoo out there, and it is going to get a whole lot worse before it gets any better. I am going to say some things that many people will probably not agree with. If you are one of those, I pray that you open your eyes to what is taking place around you.

You may be shielded from the events that are taking place in the world, but sooner or later, you will have to deal with the issues at hand.

Christ said: "But now, he that hath a purse, let him take it, and likewise his scrip: and he that hath no sword, let him sell his garment, and buy one" (Luke 22:36), and the apostle Paul wrote the following to Timothy: "But if any provide not for his own, and specially for those of his own house, he hath denied the faith, and is worse than an infidel" (1 Timothy 5:8).

The Wolves

Wolves prey on the weak.

There is also a rapidly growing number of those we call the wolves. In the animal kingdom, the wolves prey on the weak, the sick, the feeble, and the injured. In the wild, they serve the purpose of keeping herds strong, thus ensuring a strong future generation.

But when we talk about humans being wolves, we're talking about men and women who take advantage of the weak, frail, injured, and helpless people in society. These wolves are usually the deviants who resort to theft, murder, and kidnapping as a means of survival. They are the predators, and they prey upon the sheep.

In most cases, the wolves of this world are cowards, even when hunting in a pack. Stand and fight against them, show strong force, and often they will seek out a weaker form of prey.

The Sheepdogs

Sheepdogs—like the German shepherd—answer the call to defend the weak.

I am seeing a movement take place, one that I support. We are seeing a rise of just men and women answering a call. That call is to defend the weak, the innocent, the helpless, and the frail…all of those who are the sheep. The ones answering the call are the sheepdogs, who stand ready to protect the sheep if that time comes.

Having a sheepdog mentality is not about carrying a gun or some other form of weapon. It isn't about being a fifth-degree black belt, either. Criminals have guns and other weapons, and they know martial arts.

The sheepdogs are not better than the sheep; they simply realize their calling to be ready, and have the courage to take action. They have taken the time to read the writing on the wall.

In Texas, where I live, one is able to have a carry-and-conceal (C&C) license. Having a C&C does not make a person tougher or stronger. In fact, carrying a gun hasn't made me taller, more handsome, or able to leap from tall buildings—and I still can't stop trains with my bare hands. But I am a sheepdog. A sheepdog can be anyone who is prepared to protect the sheep. That is just one aspect of the sheepdog. Maybe you are a sheepdog, and you do not realize it.

Sheepdogs:

- Protect themselves, their families, and their homes with as many means as possible.
- Are prepared, knowing that a crisis situation is coming not only because they have learned from history, but because they have studied God's Word, which reveals what the future holds.
- Care for their families and are willing to do what it takes to ensure their health and welfare.
- Blend into the crowd, walk with a purpose, and are completely alert to their surroundings—before they even step outside their front doors.
- Have prepared for the coming storm, by, for example, maintaining a well-stocked pantry. They see food as an investment, and as means to help their fellow man.
- Know how the end plays out. They know that they are on the winning team, and that in the end, it is Jesus Christ they serve. They know they represent Him because it is their reasonable service to Christ, who died on the cross and shed His blood for our sins. They have submitted to Christ by living holy lives that are acceptable to Him.
- Have a strong mental fortitude, and have chosen to be the sheepdogs instead of just standing by as sheep.

Scripture tells us that there is nothing new under the sun. There will be good times and bad. Man will always repeat himself because he rarely pays attention to his past. There will always be sheep, wolves, and sheepdogs.

Sheepdogs understand fully what Christ meant in Luke 22:36, quoted earlier. It is time for the sheepdogs to recognize who they are, stand up, and start picking up the sword.

The wolves are growing in numbers—to the point that they outnumber the sheep—and it is going to get worse. The Bible couldn't be clearer concerning the truth that Christians have the right—even the duty—to defend ourselves as well as the sheep.

I live in New Braunfels, Texas, where a predator "wolf" stabbed an elderly woman in the Wal-Mart parking lot. Reading the news report about the incident infuriated both my wife and me. Had I been there, I would have instantly and without hesitation gone to the elderly woman's aid. I will protect the sheep. My wife told me that she would have gone to the woman's aid also, if given the chance.

Scripture says, "If a thief be found breaking up, and be smitten that he die, there shall no blood be shed for him" (Exodus 22:2). In other words, if a thief breaks into your house, you have the right to defend yourself, your family, and your property. It doesn't matter whether or not the thief is threatening your life. You have the right to use force—even deadly force—if need be. Did you know that our Founding Fathers based the Second Amendment (guaranteeing the right to keep and bear arms) on Scripture?

During the time of King David of Israel, every man was expected to have his own personal weapons. There were no police in those times. If an enemy was present, every man would be able to defend himself, his house, and family. If there were bands of enemies, the Israelite men could be called to arms to defend their homes. They were their own army.

Scripture says: "And David said unto his men, Gird ye on every man his sword. And they girded on every man his sword; and David also girded on his sword: and there went up after David about four hundred men; and two hundred abode by the stuff" (1 Samuel 25:13). Note here that "every man" had a sword, and when called upon, every man picked it up when it was required: "Blessed be the LORD my strength, which teacheth my hands to war, and my fingers to fight" (Psalms 144:1).

As Christians, we do not serve some limp-wristed, pacifist God like the one frequently being portrayed today. Over and over, we read in Scripture that we are to defend not only ourselves, but the weak, the innocent, the frail, and the helpless. The ancient Israelites may not have carried firearms like we have today, but they kept their weapons at their side and at the ready.

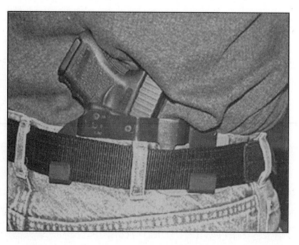

Defending one's family and home is a scriptural mandate.

As stated earlier, Jesus commanded His disciples to buy swords and strap them on. Some readers may be thinking about what Jesus said to Peter in the following account:

> Then said Jesus unto him, Put up again thy sword into his place: for all they that take the sword shall perish with the sword. Thinkest thou that I cannot now pray to my Father, and he shall presently give me more than twelve legions of angels? But how then shall the scriptures be fulfilled, that thus it must be? (Matthew 26:52–54)

Often these verses are taken out of context. But Jesus was telling Peter that the disciple would be committing suicide if he were to choose to fight. The Roman soldiers and temple guards were both able and ready to displace all of the disciples if need be, and in a moment's notice. Not only would this have been a foolish fight, but doing something like this was also undermining God's appointment for Jesus' death on the cross, His burial, and His resurrection. What Christ did at that moment was defuse a volatile situation by picking up the servant's ear and reattaching it.

Also note that Jesus told Peter to put his sword "into his place"—back at his side. Christ didn't tell Peter to throw the weapon away or to hand it over. Why would He, after He had just told His disciples to sell a coat if necessary so that they could purchase a sword?

The reason for the arms was obviously to protect the lives of the disciples, not the life of the Son of God. But more than that, it was to ensure that they could protect themselves and be able to spread the gospel freely. Not only did Christ arm the disciples with knowledge of the ways of the Lord, He taught them to protect those ways, the ways of God, and to defend themselves.

We are living in the last days of the last days. We know that our battle is not with flesh and blood, but with principalities. We, as sheepdogs, need to recognize that the time is now to stand and be willing to defend the weak, feeble, innocent, and helpless because the wolves are beginning to outnumber the sheep. If we do not stand and be ready, not only will the weak, feeble, innocent, and helpless lose, so will our ability to freely share the gospel as well.

Finally, I want to share one of my favorite verses in Scripture: "Wherefore take unto you the whole armour of God, that ye may be able to withstand in the evil day, and having done all, to stand" (Ephesians 6:13).

The "evil day" that Scripture is speaking about is upon the horizon. The time to "do all" that we can is here. We need to heed those words, knowing that we have studied God's Word and anchored them in our hearts. We must prepare ourselves physically as well, giving us the edge that God intended for us in all aspects of our existence—spiritually, mentally, and physically— "to stand."

What is your calling…sheep or sheepdog? The fact that you have made it this far into this book says that you have an interest in not being one of the sheep. Now you need to act on that desire to step up to the call to be a sheepdog by asking God to guide you in what you need in your preparedness.

chapter four

STARTING TO PREPARE STARTS WITH THE FAMILY

The key to getting prepared is to not become overwhelmed. Here's what we are facing:

- We are concerned about the end of the world as we know it.
- We want to make sure we have enough food, water, gear, and gadgets on hand to keep our families healthy, as well as be able to help loved ones in times of need.

These challenges can seem very daunting, but if you take small—what I call "baby"—steps and constantly move forward, you will be able to look back one day and see what you have done. Through perseverance and God's grace, you can put together a decent food pantry and gather ample supplies for your family (and even enough to help others).

Where to Start?

The first place to start is with your family. Sit down with them, tell them about your concerns, educate them, and guide them toward a mutual agreement. If your family is behind you, then you will be able to accomplish a lot more, much more quickly. If you do not have your family's help, it will be like walking through a muddy swamp, with each step taking its toll on you.

After getting your family's blessing and support, share this book with them. Highlight points that you will later be referring to, and ask your spouse to do the same. So often, men and women perceive the same information in two different manners. Leverage these differences in perspective as you do other issues in your marriage: by working together. There must be dialogue between family members. More ideas coming through this type of sharing are valuable; show respect for each contribution. Why do businesses have leadership meetings? They have learned the value of building upon ideas or developing existing plans in a better fashion. Working together to ensure that your family is provided for in hard times is very rewarding. My wife and I always discuss what is going on in the world, and we discuss ways we might prepare for the impact those events may have on us and our family.

Let me share with you the "hard-core" starting point of our decision to live a life of preparedness.

Hurricane Katrina and Empty Store Shelves

My wife, Tracye, and I have always tried to have a little stored away. That is just how both of us were raised. However, what really changed our lives as a married couple was when two hurricanes—Katrina and Rita—hit the Gulf Coast in 2005.

We live out in the country of southeast Texas, about two hours away from the Gulf Coast, and it is a little bit of a drive to get into town. We had been keeping an eye on the news of Katrina heading our way. She was ramping up to be a pretty bad hurricane—so much so that we realized she would probably affect us here where we live. At about nine o'clock in the evening, we headed to Wal-Mart to pick up some things we might need. In the past, when we had gone there at this time of night, the place was pretty much a "ghost mart." That night, however, that wasn't the case. It was mayhem. It seemed that everyone in our town was thinking the same: Stock up on the basic supplies like bottled water, milk, eggs, and bread.

We found some of the last bottled water on the shelves, which was six dollars for a six pack. We decided to skip that water when we found a few cases of a less-expensive brand in the sporting goods section that someone must have ditched there. While we were in the sporting goods department, we looked for flashlights and batteries—anything that would shed light. But the shelves were picked clean. There was not a single battery or flashlight to be found in the entire store.

We then looked for any sort of food that did not need to be heated, such as canned beef stew, Kraft Lunchables, or anything else along those lines. Again, the shelves were picked clean.

Next on our list: toilet paper. However, all of the toilet paper was also already gone. In fact, all the shelves had literally been cleared. Sugar, flour, potato chips, macaroni and cheese—everything was gone.

Some families there had walkie-talkies to communicate with

one another about what they had and what they still needed. They dispersed their family members, each with their shopping carts and walkie-talkies, to search for the last-minute supplies. Now these were families that had it together, even on such short notice!

Tracye and I, on the other hand, in our feeble attempt to get what we could, had to be content with what little we could find, regardless of how bad things got. I remember clearly standing in the checkout line for thirty minutes. We looked at each other and said, "Never again." We had learned a lesson, but still had a long way to go.

Right behind Katrina came Hurricane Rita. This time, we thought we were ahead of the game. At the first mention of a hurricane coming our direction, we high-tailed it over to Wal-Mart. This time around, we did better. We were able to get some bottled water, flashlights, and, yes, even toilet paper. But, even thinking that we were ahead of the game, we were still behind because there were many others like us who had apparently thought the same thing and rushed to the discount center, too.

My wife and I decided we had to get our act together. If anything serious were ever to happen, we would be like the many others out there—up the creek without a paddle. So our lives changed. We made the deliberate decision to start living a life of preparedness.

The next week, I cleaned out a closet, and we started to save water in one-gallon jugs. Every time we went to the grocery store, we picked up an extra twenty-pound bag of rice or beans. We purchased some extra cans of SPAM, or other canned goods.

We slowly started adding these things to our supply closet and, after a while, we had a nice pantry going. If we had a bad spell of weather, we would be able to get by. We also started purchasing first-aid supplies, batteries, flashlights, candles, and ammo.

Ammo? Yes! You read that right.

Because we live outside the city, if anything happens, it takes some time for the sheriff to respond. Again, it is better to be prudent than to be caught off guard, so I started to put away .22-rimfire and .12-gauge-shotgun ammunition since those were the only firearms we had.

We thought we had all of our needs covered, that is, until the H1N1 swine flu epidemic hit in the spring of 2009 and our little town was ground zero for the outbreak here in Texas.

H1N1 Mexican Flu/Swine Flu: Our Town, Ground Zero for Texas Flu Threat Rises; 100 New Cases in New Braunfels, TX

In less than twenty-four hours, a hundred more cases of suspected swine flu were detected in Comal County. Comal County Health Authority Dorothy Overman said Wednesday the majority of flu cases were in students and the decision to close schools as well as "social distancing" could prevent the further spread of influenza. [14]

That was the news we woke up to on April 30, 2009. At around 9 PM April 29, we had crossed the threshold for the definition of a Phase 6, global pandemic with the World Health Organization (WHO) declaration. This had not happened in any of our lives so far. We were in uncharted territory.

It was suggested that people avoid public gatherings, shopping, school, etc. Many businesses, as well as all the schools, closed down. Our sleepy little town turned into a ghost town.

People were told to avoid going to the emergency room if they thought they had been exposed or were symptomatic. Nearby hospitals were becoming extremely overwhelmed. The flu was coming in waves—and the waves were getting bigger.

It appeared that this flu produces a distinctive hoarseness in many victims. The symptoms, in general, match those of other flus, namely: sore throat, body aches, headache, cough, and fever. Some have all these symptoms, while others may have only one or two.

At ten o'clock, an hour after the WHO announcement, Tracye and I headed to Wal-Mart, figuring that the scare related to the emergency declaration would keep folks at home. Again, we were surprised. The shelves were already missing items like hand sanitizer, face masks, Lysol, and vitamins.

Due to the prior events, we had already started stocking up on things to tide us over if we needed to stay inside for a while, but we were not fully stocked up on medical supplies. We had a few things on hand, but we could have been better prepared.

Going through this H1N1 outbreak gave us yet another wake-up call concerning what we needed to work on next. We needed to have even more supplies on hand. We were hearing that many of the local pharmacies and hospitals were already running out of Tamiflu and Relenza, the standard treatments for the flu. So the next day, we went to our local pharmacy to buy some Sambucol (also known as Sambucus), an elderberry extract invented in Israel that studies have shown helps prevent or overcome the flu. That day, I purchased the last two bottles at our drug store.

As a side note and personal endorsement, I have seen

Sambucol in action. Every time a member of my family has had any symptoms of the flu or a fever, I have immediately started the whole family on it. Usually within twenty-four hours, there are no more symptoms. I keep dosing everyone for another day or two. Within that time-frame, the whole family is on their feet and doing great. So although I am not a doctor, I would advise keeping a couple bottles of Sambucol on hand.

Oscillococinum, a homeopathic remedy, has also been proven as quite effective in a large clinical trial in Europe with an H1N1 variant. This product can be found in many health food stores as well as some pharmacies.

In my research of flu pandemics, history shows that the flu first attacks the community through contact with others. Then a process takes place: First, many people get sick. Then there is a scare, and everyone stays inside their homes. After several weeks to a month—long enough for most of the symptoms to subside—people start feeling better again. So they hurry back to work, even though they are not completely recovered and are still sick enough to pass the weakened flu along. According to the history accounts that I've read, the odds are very good that within three to six months, the flu will come back with a vengeance.

Knowing this, over time, my wife and I worked on fine tuning our supplies for the next wave of the flu. Because of the national attention on the flu epidemic, people here were careful and the doctors were doing a good job. So, ultimately, we didn't experience another wave.

I've shared these stories in hopes that you learn from them. It took two hurricanes for us to realize what we needed to do. The key is to work together with your spouse. You will be amazed at what a husband and wife can do when they have a shared goal.

You will also find that as you prepare for the worst, your family will grow stronger in its relationship and family unity.

Why Prepare?

Ask 101 folks why they are preparing, and you will hear 101 different reasons. But the reason I wrote this book—my "why?"—is so that my family and I can make a difference for the Lord.

As I have said, I do not anticipate some type of *Mad Max* scenario taking place. There will be chaos and disruption, but within thirty to ninety days, most people will start settling down into the New Normal.

What do you think is most important when it comes to preparedness? I bet nine out of ten readers would answer "family." I think this is what makes a Christian who prepares for hard times different. I see us as "little Noahs" preparing our arks so that we and our families will see another day during world-changing difficulties. But food and gear alone are not going to get us through. Our spiritual preparedness will have a lot to do with whether we make it or not. Our relationship with the Lord reflects our concern for ensuring our families' health and welfare, and our love for Him binds the family more tightly together during those hard times. Our love for Him helps us get through the thick and thin; our spiritual fortitude toughens us so that we can face tomorrow. Knowing the Lord is right with us is what helps us weather the storms.

Unfortunately, those who have a fear-based mentality will not make it. Without a positive outlook, then what is already a crazy world will become a whole lot worse. Man's very nature is to self destruct. Facing hardship with a negative attitude usually causes one of two things to happen:

1. One is likely to resort to a life of crime and become a predator upon society.

2. One is likely to resort to drugs, drinking, and other vices to fill the void that God would occupy. During a time of hardship, this void becomes even more painful and the ability to cope with difficult situations diminishes. So the person delves even further into self-destructive abuse of the vice, which can be deadly.

You need a "why," a deep "why"—not some excuse like "the little green men are coming and I need to prepare." This does not have the depth of spirit that will give you the grit to carry on day by day. A good "why" is, "I'm preparing so that I can provide peace of mind, health, and welfare for my family." This becomes your foundation, but you need to build upon it. For example, we see ourselves as being effective for the Lord during the coming hard days. I do not have faith in today's lukewarm, sugar-coated pastors who have no idea what the Bible really says. So I see that we, as "laymen" and "laywomen," need to take up the cross and share the gospel with a hurting nation. We can build upon our own "why" foundation by always being ready to share the hope of our Lord Jesus Christ (see 1 Peter 3:15).

This is why I do not see a *Mad Max* or an *I Am Legend* outcome. Hatred and fear drain the average person: They do not motivate us to move forward. If anything, they hold us back. What hatred and fear provide are just temporary attitude changes, kind of like a passing caffeine high after drinking too much coffee. That empty burst of energy will drive us for a few hours, but it is hard to maintain. You know how you feel once you come down off of a caffeine high? It's the same when you allow fear and hatred to drive you…you feel drained. It is a proven fact that man cannot maintain that level of functionality and awareness before he finally runs out of steam. Hatred and fear are only temporary motivators and thus only provide temporary satisfaction.

The foundation of true preparedness requires long-term solutions, thus the deep "why," backed up by our relationship with the Lord, will drive us when we do not want to get out of bed, or when we just want to give up, period.

This is why those of us who are Bible-believing Christians need to strengthen and nourish our spiritual muscles. When the evil day comes, we will be able to stand.

So, ask yourself, "Why do we want to have extra water on hand?" "Why do we feel the need to learn self-defense and own a gun?" "Why do we want to gain more knowledge regarding survival skills and medical care?" Constantly reminding yourself of the deep "why" will empower you to keep moving forward.

Preventing Overwhelming Burnout

With baby steps, one can accomplish just about anything at any given time. I am a big fan of taking baby steps, and I am always asking the Lord to guide me down the paths my wife and I should take.

I want to share with you what my wife and I consider our "life" Bible verse: "Trust in the LORD with all thine heart; and lean not unto thine own understanding. In all thy ways acknowledge him, and he shall direct thy paths" (Proverbs 3:5–6). I call this our "life verse" because we both try hard daily to live by these very words, trusting God always, never leaning on our own understanding, and knowing that, in doing that, God will direct our paths. Peace comes from having Him at the helm.

However, here is some bad news: If you have not taken any steps toward preparedness, your baby steps will have to pick up the pace a bit to catch up.

Priority 1: Secure Your Food and Water Supply

I have provided a basic list of food staples for a family of four on the next page. This list is only a suggestion, a minor foundation to build upon. Some things are probably on this list that you do not need or even eat, but there may be other ideas that you can use.

PREP TIP—Only purchase food you eat regularly. Children will just about starve themselves before they will eat foods they despise. So, for example, if you and your kids never eat oatmeal, and in fact if all of you hate oatmeal, don't buy it just because it is on the list.

Where to Store Your Food

Before you start purchasing all of your food supplies, you'll need to find a suitable place to house all that food. There are certain conditions that you need to think about. For example, food does not do well when exposed to heat and light. Where my family and I live, our garage is not air-conditioned, and it actually gets hotter in the garage than the ambient temperature outside…which does not create good storage space. So you will need to determine what area will be best to properly store your food.

Food and Water Storage List for a Family of Four

Grains

Wheat—600 lb.

Flour—100 lb.

Corn meal—100 lb.

Oats—100 lb.

Rice—200 lb.

Pasta—100 lb.

Sugars

Honey—12 lb.

Sugar—160 lb.

Brown sugar—12 lb.

Molasses—4 lb.

Corn syrup—12 lb.

Jams—12 lb.

Powdered fruit drinks—24 lb.

Flavored gelatins—4 lb.

Legumes

Beans, dry—120 lb.

Lima beans—20 lb.

Soy beans—40 lb.

Split peas—20 lb.

Lentils—20 lb.

Dry soup mix—20 lb.

Milk

Dry milk—240 lb.

Evaporated milk—48 cans

Non-fat/low-fat dry milk—52 lb.

Cooking Essentials

Baking powder—4 lb.

Baking soda—4 lb.

Yeast—2 lb.

Salt—20 lb.

Vinegar—2 gal.

Water—1460 gal.

Bleach—4 gal.

Shortening—16 lb.

Vegetable oil—8 gal.

Mayonnaise—8 qt.

Salad dressing—4 qt.

Peanut butter—16 lb.

You will also want to think about convenience. If you keep your food in a closet upstairs and the kitchen is downstairs, common sense says that you will have to hike up and down the stairs often. Breaking up your food storage areas may be a good solution. The closer you can locate your food storage area to your kitchen, the easier you will find it to rotate the food storage. Storing food is not hard, but it can be time-consuming. If it becomes too much of a hassle and if you are the average person, you will burn out sooner or later, your food preparations will taper off, and eventually you will quit.

Finding the Best Conditions for Food Storage

As I mentioned, store your food in a cool, dry place away from sunlight and in an area that maintains a pretty constant temperature reading of around 60–70 degrees Fahrenheit. If the temperature is too cold, the food may freeze, and if it is too hot, it will lose nutritional value.

One of the coolest spots in your home may be in a basement, which is often the best place for food storage. Be sure to keep the food away from any heat source if you have a central heater or furnace.

If you live in the country or in a rural area and you have a root cellar, then you have been truly blessed. Insulated, temperature-controlled garages are also a great place for food storage, as are spare bedrooms, unfinished rooms, crawl spaces, closets, under stairways, and even under beds.

Ideas for Tight Quarters and Apartment Dwellers

One of the projects I have produced for my website readers is a DVD entitled *TEOTWAWKI* (an acronym for "the end of the world as we know it"). This data DVD, full of files, articles, lectures, and other tidbits of information, is available at the Prophezine online store at http://www.prophezine.com. Many people purchased this and loved the information. But, I received many emails from people who live in apartments or small residences with no extra space. As a result, I produced another data DVD geared specifically to those who live in the city. It gives some great ideas on how and where to store one's food supply.

If you live in a small house where space is very limited, that doesn't mean you can't prepare for at least short-term emergencies by storing extra food and supplies. In fact, if you look at it as something fun and even make a game out of it, you can almost make your food storage "disappear" with a simple sheet, a lamp, and maybe a small bunch of flowers. By doing this, you can create a quick end table that looks good—and no one visiting your home will even know it is a stack of food.

Here are some other ideas for food storage in areas with limited space:

Under the bed—Because the space under most beds is usually empty or full of unwanted junk, it can be a good place to store cases of food like #10 cans of fruits, veggies, or even dehydrated/freeze-dried food. The canned goods from the grocery store, such as green beans and corn, fit nicely under beds also.

PREP TIP—If you purchase cases of canned goods from the grocery store, talk to the department manager and ask for a discount; you may be surprised how much off the regular store shelf price you will get.

Now you can either just slide the cases under the bed frame or—even better—put the mattress right in top of the cases of food. Because cases of cans stack nicely, you could create a large stockpile of canned goods under a single mattress. To disguise this, simply cover the boxes with a dust ruffle. Be sure to label each box with a thick, black marking pen so you can read what each case contains without pulling it out from under the bed. It is also a good idea to keep a master list of what you have on hand and where everything is stored. Only store the items that you won't be using in the near future under your bed or in the more out-of-the-way storage spaces.

In bottom shelves of bookcases—If you are like me, you probably have stuff on the bottom shelves of your bookcases that you never touch. This is also a good place to store your canned goods or #10 cans. Clean out those areas out and use them for storage.

Make a bookshelf—This is an old college-student trick. Using your cases of food, put a couple stacks of cases on the floor, then put a pine wood plank atop those two stacks. You can get the wood planks pretty cheaply at your local hardware store. They are usually cut in four- or six-foot lengths, and are ready to be used as shelves. Put more cases on top of the ends of the pine plank and then add another plank. Keep going up until you have reached a comfortable height that is still stable.

End tables and coffee tables—If you have stored your food in five- or six-gallon buckets, you can make end tables or coffee tables out of these as well. The hardware stores sell round pieces of wood that are pretty much furniture-ready. All you need to do is put these on top of the bucket, cover it with a tablecloth or piece of fabric, and you have created a piece of furniture!

Storing water—I have advised many folks not to throw away the one-gallon jugs that juice and water come in. Reuse them and fill with water. If you are like us, you really do not have much stored under the bathroom sinks. This is a great place to store your jugs of water.

The thing about storing one-gallon jugs is that you can store them all over the place…in closets, under sinks, in chests, under beds, under desks and other furniture, on bottom shelves, on top of the refrigerator, and many other places. Look for unused storage areas, and then take advantage of that space by storing your water there.

Commercial Products That Help

The preparedness industry has grown, and in today's world, many great products out there can really make a difference in your food and water preparations. I want to introduce to you some of these products—these are ones we use that have helped greatly.

Food Storage Shelving Systems

When you start storing food, one big factor is rotating your food. It is a drag to pull out a can of beans that is over six years old! Nothing is probably wrong with food that old, as long as the can has maintained its integrity, but the nutritional value is probably pretty low after that length of time in storage. Shelf Reliance has produced a great shelf-management system. Its largest free-stand-ing shelf will store and rotate more than 450 cans of food in a 72" x 24.5" x 36.5" space. The company's patented, front-loading technology automatically rotates cans on a first-in, first-out basis, always ensuring that the food is rotated properly—with very little effort.

Front-loading shelves ensure proper rotation.

Shelf Reliance also offers smaller shelves that fit nicely into closets, laundry rooms, or other out-of-the-way areas. Further, for those with limited space, it sells a "Cansolidator Pantry Plus—a front-loading system that automatically rotates up to sixty cans. These can be placed in your existing cupboards and are completely adjustable to fit your specifically sized shelf. They are expandable and even stackable. This is a great food-storage system that takes the hassle out of rotating your cans and allows you to organize cans the way you want. For example, you can purchase a week's worth of food and plan your meals. You can then put your cans into the unit so that, say, the cans for Monday's meal come out first, the cans for Tuesday's meal come out second, and so forth.

Shelf Reliance products are easy to assemble. Visit http://gano. shelfreliance.com/ to find out more, and to take advantage of a 20–25-percent discount.

Berkey water filtration system

Water Filtration Systems

There you are: The world is in turmoil, and you have no electricity. But more importantly, you have no running water. What do you do now? If you have a water filtering system, you can go to the local pool, stream, or even the tank of your toilet and get water to filter. Then you have life-sustaining water to drink.

The Berkey water filtration systems are a great solution for large families—you can break them down for travel, use them at outdoor activities, and best of all, use them during unexpected emergencies. The systems purify both treated water and untreated, raw water from such sources as remote lakes, streams, and even stagnant ponds. These are the perfect water filtration systems to have, especially when the electricity goes out or when your treated water may not be available.

My own personal preference is the Royal Berkey system, which removes pathogenic bacteria, cysts, and parasites entirely, as well as extracts harmful chemicals such as herbicides, pesticides, organic solvents, radon 222, and trihalomethanes.

The system also reduces nitrates, nitrites, and unhealthy minerals such as lead and mercury. This system is so powerful that it can remove red food coloring from water without eliminating the beneficial minerals. Constructed of highly polished stainless steel, it has a storage capacity of about 3.25 gallons, stands around twenty-three inches high, and is about nine and one-half inches round. The upper chamber sits within a lower chamber for moving, and it stands only a little over fifteen inches tall.

Normally, the system is configured with two purification elements and will purify up to four gallons (15.1 liters) in approximately an hour. The nice thing about the Royal Berkey is that it can be expanded to use four water filters, bumping up the capability to purify eight gallons of water in approximately an hour's time.

The company also offers a portable water purifier, which is basically a sports water bottle that contains a smaller water filter. I like the Sport Berkey because it is portable and will filter a good amount of water—about 150 gallons of raw water and more than six hundred gallons of municipal water out of the tap. The bare minimum is one gallon per person per day, but with a water source and the bottle, you can increase that and stay nicely hydrated, even in a bad situation.

Berkey Water products are available from Survivor Mall (www. survivormall.com) or The Berkey Guy (www.directive21.com).

Food Dehydrators

Why do you need a food dehydrator? Because dehydrated food:

Saves Money—The foremost reason to purchase a food dehydrator is to save money. I buy food when it is in season and at the lowest prices. I then bring it home, cut it up, and put it in the food dehydrator. By purchasing food in bulk, I save about 50 percent over the regular price.

Dehydrated food saves money, saves space, preserves nutrients, and tastes great.

Whenever we have leftovers, I always dehydrate them. In fact, one of the best tips I have discovered is dehydrating the salsa I make when guests come over. The recipe I have is large—and there is always some left over. I put the leftover salsa on a specially lined tray and dehydrate it, then crush it up and run it through a blender to turn it into a powder. The result is a great spicy tomato powder that I can shake onto any food to make it explode with a delicious, spicy flavor.

In a TEOTWAWKI situation, rice, beans, and lentils will get pretty boring very quickly. Having the means to kick the meal up with spices and rubs made in the dehydrator will be important.

Tastes Great—The process of drying out food concentrates the flavor. For example, I can slice tomatoes, then sprinkle the slices with salt, pepper, and other spices. Deydration turns these into a form of a "tomato chip" that is full of flavor.

Another delicious idea is to dehydrate sliced peaches with some cinnamon and sugar (or just leave it as is). The peach comes out of the dehydrator as a crunchy chip. The flavor is concentrated, and these make great snacks for the kids.

Saves Space—Dehydrated foods are small in size, thus easy to store. A large bag of carrots, after dehydration, will fit into a quart-sized mason jar. Like other dehydrated items, the carrots will have a concentrated taste, and if you add an oxygen absorber (those little packets you find in packages to keep items dry and fresh) to the jar, the carrots will last several years. You can vacuum seal dehydrated food in bags or freeze it for easy storage.

Preserves Nutrients—Dehydrating food helps preserve nutrients and enzymes with no additives or preservatives. You can make your own beef jerky that will retain the flavor as well as the protein and nutrients without any of the preservatives found in store-bought beef jerky.

My personal recommendation is the Excalibur 2900, nine-tray dehydrator. Here is what the Excalibur website has to say about it:

> European styled unit, great for year round counter use. Large enough for quantity drying. 9 trays with 15 square feet of drying area. 1¼" of clearance between shelves. Weight limit per shelf: 12 pounds.
>
> The Excalibur 9-Tray Food Dehydrator includes a 24-page instruction manual with tips on getting started with your new Excalibur Dehydrator, how to prepare your foods for dehydration, and recipes for dehydrating jerky, nuts, raisin bread, pasta, yogurt, cheese, and even drying photos.
>
> Turbo Charged Parallexx Horizontal-Airflow Drying System. Complete drying system in rear (includes thermostat and fan). The Parallexx design, with a temperature controlled, fan forced, horizontal drying system mounted in the rear is exclusive to the 2000 and higher Series. The same features found in Excalibur's USDA-approved, $3500 commercial model…in an affordable home unit. Cool air is drawn in the back, heated, and distributed

evenly across each tray. During the dehydration process, warm air removes moisture from foods and is pushed out the front of the machine.

- Easy to clean…Spills fall on seamless bottom. Flexible mesh tray inserts (Polyscreens) hold food above the tray frames.
- Horizontal drying provides even drying, eliminating tray re-stacking. Fast drying…you don't lose heat because you don't have to take your Excalibur apart to change the tray sequence.
- Adjustable thermostat allows perfect drying every time. Range: 85º–145º F. The adjustable thermostat can be set for a specific temperature, in increments of 5º F.
- Square design increases drying area 25% with no holes in center of tray. The square design makes it easy to spread puree for fruit leathers and rollups, using Paraflexx Food Drying Sheets, plastic wrap, or parchment paper tray liners.
- Versatile…Trays can be removed to expand drying chamber.
- Removable door and trays—An Excalibur does not have to be taken completely apart to check drying or add more food. Each tray rests on its own support, making it easy to slide each one in and out, as needed. Especially useful when removing thinner slices that finished drying first. It only takes a few seconds to check a tray, thus your food doesn't have time to cool to any material degree.

Almost unbreakable, and FDA-approved polycarbonate trays. Excalibur trays are dishwasher safe.[15]

Why Excalibur?

Using forced air is the best way to get evenly dehydrated food. I have owned those round, stackable dehydrators that have an element at the bottom—but all those do is cook the food, not dehydrate it. Sure, these types of units "dehydrate" food, but the goal is to retain as many nutrients as possible. Utilizing a forced-air unit—with temperature control—is the way to go. This way, you are getting as close to having "raw food" as you can get—without cooking away all the nutrients.

The Excalibur is one of the best kitchen items my wife and I have purchased to date. During the growing seasons, we keep our dehydrator going all the time, preparing all kinds of fruits and veggies.

In fact, here is a great snack tip: If you have plenty of tomatoes, squash, or zucchini, thinly cut them, sprinkle with seasoning salt, and place them in your dehydrator. When they're done, they will be as thin as potato chips and nicely seasoned. Our family likes the dehydrated tomatoes the best.

My family and I have been able to expand our food storage pantry because of our food dehydrator. We are able to prepare flavored rice, beans, lentils, pasta, and other dry food items. One great idea for preparing dehydrated food is to place all the items into a cast iron pot, then add water and spices. Set the pot outside or in a warm space for several hours. All the water, dehydrated foods, and spices will turn into a healthy, tasty meal that you don't have to spend hours cooking. If you have a solar oven, this dish will taste even better. The cost of food, as well as the fact that it doesn't take any gas or electricity to cook it, makes this meal cost just pennies. You don't have even have to be living in an "end-of-the-world" scenario to make a meal that is good for your family, tastes great, and costs very little. But, if you are living a preparedness lifestyle, it sure helps the pocketbook in the long run. I recommend purchasing the Excalibur dehydrator from Ultimate Nourishment at www.ultimate-weight-products.com. At the time of this writing, customers could use the code "VIPCUSTOMER" to receive a 5 percent discount.

Kitchen Mill

A kitchen mill will expand your family's diet and your ability to produce more items from the staples in your food storage.

I have this on my list of must-have food-storage prep items because wheat can be stored up to twenty-five years. In fact, wheat was found in King Tut's tomb that was still in good enough condition to grind into flour and use in bread. The nutritional value of the flour was probably nil, with the wheat being that old, but the wheat was still in an edible state and was not rotten.

The Blend-Tec Kitchen Mill has to be one of the best and least-expensive grain mills on the market today. It is a work horse, and has a lifetime warranty on the milling chamber and mill pan. All electric grain mills are very noisy—they sound like a huge shop vac running in your kitchen—but the Blend-Tec is not as noisy as the others, at least in my experience. Another thing I like about the Blend-Tec Kitchen Mill is that it uses a stoneless milling process, reducing the heat that normally destroys nutrients. The micronetic chamber of the mill "bursts" the grains of wheat into impressively fine flour.

Because it is somewhat noisy, it's good for the milling of the grain to be quick. The Blend-Tec mills up to one pound of grain in a minute, which is pretty fast. The wheat-to-flour ratio is about one cup of wheat to one and one-half cups of flour. When the wheat is being milled, it is shot into an air-tight pan that holds twenty-four cups of milled flour. This means that you will not have flour dust floating all over the kitchen after you are finished. Other types of grain mills shoot the flour over to another container, so they lose flour and tend to be messy. The Blend-Tec mill has a great rubber seal that locks onto the milling portion and creates an air tight seal, thus no messy flour to clean up afterwards.

Upkeep on the Blend-Tec mill is pretty easy. It comes with a small cleaning brush, but I recommend using a natural-hair paint brush that you use only for cleaning your grain mill, which cleans it much faster. The nice thing is that the milling chamber is self-cleaning and service-free, whereas other types of mills usually must be disassembled for cleaning. Finally, the Blend-Tec has five different texture settings, which means you aren't limited to milling wheat alone. You can mill rice, soybeans, popcorn, and legumes, which other mills can't even touch. This will expand your family's diet and your ability to produce more items from the staples in your food storage. While the Blend-Tec mill can grind any bean, legume, or grain (except coffee beans), as long as they are dry, it is not recommended to grind nuts, spices, or spelt. The Blend-Tec Kitchen Grain Mill can grind items with up to 15 percent oil or 18 percent moisture. So even with these very minor limitations, the Blend-Tec Kitchen Grain Mill is an excellent prepper item to have in your kitchen.

Needless to say, with a kitchen mill, you can make a lot of flour, which in turn makes a lot of bread, flatbread, tortillas, cakes, muffins, etc., at a very low price. All of these dry-good items have a storage shelf life of at least fifteen years. So by owning a kitchen mill, you can produce healthy food items that have no preservatives, additives, dyes, etc., for your family—for only pennies.

The Blend-Tec mill is also available from Ultimate Nourishment, at www.ultimate-weight-products.com, where you can check into whether the VIPCUSTOMER code for a 5 percent discount may still be valid.

Vacuum-Seal Packaging System

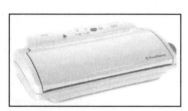

Extend the freshness of food with a vacuum sealer.

Vacuum-packing keeps food fresh in the freezer for months—without freezer burn. The FoodSaver V2440 Vacuum-Packaging System, with a two-step process of removing air and then sealing the bag, is one of my favorite kitchen prepper tools because there are so many things you can do with it.

Meat, chicken, fish, vegetables, and fruit will stay fresh in the freezer for months, even years. Make an entire plate of food, or vacuum-package last night's pizza to eat months later. It is that good.

Even better is that I've discovered many other ways to use the FoodSaver that have nothing to do with food!

For example:

- Vacuum seal a bag of bandages, gauze, single-use Neosporin packs, hand sanitizer towels, or pretty much anything you would want in an emergency first-aid pack to keep in your car, backpack, bug-out bag, or just about anywhere.
- Vacuum seal a bag of important documents, pictures, coins, jewelry, or anything else of value.
- Put a can of sardines, a breakfast bar or two, instant coffee, sugar, creamer, mustard, and ketchup packets, instant pasta meals, or some other instant meal, and put all of the items into a vacuum-sealed bag for your own homemade MRE—Meal Ready to Eat.
- Assemble a cache of money, barter items, ammo, knife, a change of clothes, and even a handgun, then seal all of those items in a bag and store in a safe spot for later retrieval.

I use my vacuum sealer for storing much of my dehydrated foods. I also drop in an oxygen absorber to keep the food from going bad, because oxygen is one of the top enemies of keeping food fresh as well as of food staying dry and crisp.

There are 101 different uses for the FoodSaver 2440, but also great are the attachments available to expand its use. For example, a jar-sealing attachment for both large-mouth and com-mon-mouth mason jars is an excellent way to vacuum seal dry goods. In fact, a really neat thing to do is get a one-quart mason jar and put in beans, rice, lentils, soup mix, dehydrated carrots, peppers, corn, okra, or any other vegetables, then drop an oxygen absorber into the jar along with the soup makings, pop on a lid, and vacuum seal. You could even cut a piece of decorative cloth to go over the lid, add a label and a card, and you have a great gift. Or forget all the fancy stuff and create your own soups, ready to go. Just pour the contents into a pot and add water; a couple of hours later, you will have soup.

You can also purchase in bulk some of your favorite nuts and make a nut mix in a vacuum-sealed jar. Again, this makes a nice gift as well as being a great way to expand your food storage pantry.

The FoodSaver system offers pre-cut bags you can purchase, as well as rolls of material to make your own bags. To do that, you seal one end and cut to size the bag you need. This is great when you want to seal really big items such as a whole deer leg, a whole salmon, or other fish. You can even use the vacuum sealer to prevent your hunting rifle from rusting if you are going to a wet area. It will remain safe and dry while in transit, and you will have a clean, rust-free hunting rifle when you arrive to your hunting camp in the woods. The best places to purchase the FoodSaver are Wal-Mart, which usually has them at a good price, or through Amazon—www.amazon.com—where, many times, the seller pays the shipping.

Pressure Cooker/Canner

One thing many people forget when prepping their food storage is having adequate protein. Some good sources are soy beans, lentils, and such, but nothing beats meat. Of all the pressure cookers/canners on the market, the All American Pressure Canner 921,

A pressure cooker/canner is an essential tool for long-term food storage.

twenty-one quart model, is probably the most popular. It is large enough to can a lot of jars, but not so big that you can't cook dinner in it. With the All American 921, you can safely can meat, fish, poultry, all kinds of vegetables, and more. If you are a hunter, this is also a great tool for roasting deer or elk; it makes these tough cuts of meat really tender.

Another great benefit of the All American 921 is that there are no rubber gaskets because it features an exclusive, precision-machined, "metal-to-metal" sealing system. When you place the lid on the pot, the "positive-action clamping locks" align the cover to the base, forming a steam tight seal. Care for this is very simple; just rub some olive oil around the rim. Also, because it does not have a rubber gasket, the cover always opens and closes easily. This is really a no-frills tool, but one that will really help with long-term food storage.

For example: You can purchase chicken thighs in the bag at a relatively inexpensive price. Get a big bag of these, skin and debone them, and then put the chicken meat in hot sterilized jars. Top the contents off with broth, and place the jars in the cooker/canner. Cook at ten pounds for an hour and fifteen minutes, and then you will have canned chicken that is cooked and ready to serve. It is really that easy.

I recommend getting the All American through Amazon at www.amazon.com, which, as of this writing, offered it for about thirty-five dollars less than what other merchants were charging. In addition, Amazon frequently offers free shipping. Check the website for more details.

Recommended Commercial Food Products

Rule #1: Eat what you buy and buy what you eat. There is no time like today to get started purchasing your food preps.

Most people don't realize that you don't need the fancy, freeze-dried food that lasts through a nuclear attack. You don't need cases of military MREs or anything like that. Most canned foods today will easily last a year if you store them in a cool, dry place. Often canned food will last a lot longer than the "sell by" date. As long as the can itself is not compromised, the food inside should be good to eat. The nutritional value might decrease with age, but it is still edible.

Now I want to focus on some products that are good to keep around.

Powdered Drink Mixes (Gatorade, Kool-Aid, Lipton Iced Tea mix, Tang, etc.)

It's important to keep drink mixes on hand for several reasons. First, in an extended crisis, you will get sick of drinking water very quickly. Second, drink mixes have sugar and other ingredients to help you hydrate faster and replenish your nutrients as well as electrolytes. These products store easily for a couple of years as long as you keep them away from moisture, and as long as the inner seals are not broken.

Powdered Milk

Having powdered milk around is a must. Milk is a key ingredient in many recipes, as well as in foods such as cheese and whipping cream. Plus, if you have kids, powdered milk is important for their health and nutrition. When storing powdered milk, give some thought to where you will store it. Powdered milk does best in 60–70-degree Fahrenheit temperatures; it not keep well in heat, so storing it in tall cabinets, the garage, or a hot laundry room is not a good idea. If the milk is exposed to heat, it will "cook," and instead of a cream-colored powder, you will have a brownish mix. The heat eventually affects the taste and nutritional value of the milk as well.

Tuna and Chicken (Foil Pouches)

Recently, more and more companies have been moving from packing chicken and tuna in cans to selling them in foil pouches. I personally like these because they offer the same quantity of meat, but are easier to store. In fact, many of the brand-name meat pouches have a hole at the top of the packaging so you can hang these from a long nail inside a cupboard or closet. The technology behind these foil pouches allows them to be stored for a decent period of time—and because you do not need a can opener, eating on the go and right out of the pouch is really convenient.

SPAM

The king of survival food! If you want something that will last through a nuclear attack, SPAM is it. When talking about the pressure cooker/canner, I mentioned that often preppers forget about the protein intake needed, but more importantly, they forget about storing foods with appropriate fat content.

What? Fat?

Yes, in this day and age of being hit from all sides about the negatives of fat, fat is needed in a survival situation. In fact, you can die if you do not get fat in your diet—but SPAM provides a great source of both fat and protein, and it will last for years. I recommend getting different types of SPAM for variety, including the regular, low-sodium, bacon, smoked, spicy, and turkey flavors.

Canned Whole Chicken and Other Canned Meats

A whole cooked chicken in a can? Yes, they do make these, and they are rather inexpensive. You can get ham in a can as well. In fact many of the "dollar" stores sell canned hams for just one dollar. What a great purchase! As I said, protein is often overlooked, so any sort of canned meat is good to have in your food storage.

Canned Pastas

I am a big fan of canned pasta, and it comes in all kinds of shapes and sizes, from ravioli to spaghetti. Most cans have pull-top lids, so no can openers are needed. The nice thing about canned pasta is that it comes in large, twenty-six and forty-eight-ounce cans. This makes a quick dinner and is a good source of carbohydrates. In a TEOTWAKI situation, you will be burning the carbs pretty fast. This sort of food will help replenish those carbs and keep you on your feet, running strong.

Dinty Moore Beef Stews

Like the canned pastas, Dinty Moore Beef Stew and Dinty Moore Chicken & Dumplings are good products to have on hand. Each can will easily feed two people or stuff one person to the brim. They also come in a forty-eight-ounce can and have a pull top lid. With the Dinty Moore Stew products, you get your meat and veggies as well as a good source of carbohydrates, and they are good meals to have in stressful times. Warm them up right in the can, and you have a bit of Grandma's house right there. A warm meal like this is a good motivator, too.

Canned Tamales

Tamales are corn meal tubes filled with chili-spiced meat. They are usually wrapped in corn husks and steamed. They are a great ethnic dish that helps break up the boredom of bland prep food. In fact, cook up some rice and beans from your storage, and you will have a great Mexican dinner. Make some quick tortillas, and you will be totally set. These come in a standard, sixteen-ounce can as well as larger cans.

Canned Beans (Pork and Beans, Barbecue Beans, Texas Beans, etc.)

Beans...the magical fruit. Canned beans are a great product to have around. They range from small, four-ounce, single children's serving cans all the way up to #10 cans. Cooked beans are a great meal all in themselves. Bake up a fresh loaf of bread— better yet, corn bread—and you will have a tummy-filler of a meal. Rehydrate some dried meat, or add some hot dogs you have frozen, and kick the beans up a notch. Canned beans are inexpensive, and there are many different ways they have been prepared in the can—from a sweet, Boston-baked bean to a spicy, Texas-chili style. This is a great way to add variety to your family's food.

Potatoes (Instant Mashed, Potato Buds, Potato Flakes)

Potatoes are another great addition to your preps, and often they are very inexpensive as well. Instant potatoes are quick to cook, and you can spice them up just about any way you wish. They are a great source of carbohydrates when you and your family may be doing chores in the yard and getting that garden ready. You can use them to make potato pancakes for breakfast or even for dinner. Mashed potatoes make an excellent soup thickener as well. Spread some ground beef, mixed veggies, and a layer of mashed potatoes in a casserole dish, and repeat the layering until you fill the dish for a very filling shepherd's pie. Instant mashed potatoes need to be part of your pantry, if for no other reason than they are a great tummy filler.

Sweetened Condensed Milk

When I was growing up and our family did not have much money, on cold mornings, my mom would open a can of sweetened condensed milk, pour it in a pot, add water to thin it out, and stir in some cocoa powder for a great-tasting, hot cocoa drink. It was thick and sweet, and for as little as a dollar a can, you can't go wrong. You can do all kinds of things with sweetened condensed milk. In fact, you can pour it over almost any grain you have boiled to make a great breakfast, or you can chill the entire dish to make a delicious dessert. Putting sweetened condensed milk in a pitcher and adding water also makes a sweet milk you can use for everyday drinking.

Before the nineteenth century, drinking milk was an iffy situation because of health risks. Milk that came straight from the cow was loaded with bacteria. Milk not consumed within a matter of hours in summertime soon spoiled in the heat. Illness, allegedly derived from contaminated milk consumption, was referred to as "the milk-sick," "milk poison," "the slows," "the trembles," and "the milk evil." Granted, some of these illnesses (considering modern-day knowledge of lactose intolerance) were probably not due to the milk, but the stigma persisted. The idea for a portable canned milk product that would not spoil came to Gail Borden during a transatlantic trip in 1852. The cows in the hold of the ship became too seasick to be milked during the long trip, and an immigrant infant died from lack of milk. Borden realized his goal in 1854. His first condensed milk product lasted three days without souring. He first thought the condensing process of the milk made it more stable, but later realized it was the heating process that killed the bacteria and microorganisms that cause spoilage.

Borden was granted a patent for sweetened condensed milk in 1856. The sugar was added to inhibit bacterial growth.[16]

Sweetened milk is a great product to have on hand for many reasons, and it is actually cheaper than regular milk you get at the store.

Canned Fruit and Vegetables

It is always good to have canned fruit and vegetables on hand. Fruit cocktail is always a favorite with kids, and it comes in #10 cans as well. Peas, green beans, corn, and other canned veggies are always good to keep on hand no matter what the situation. My wife and I like mandarin oranges, peaches, and pineapple, so we always keep a lot of these on hand. Need a little extra something to round out lunch or dinner? Just crack open a can of fruit. Need to add something special to the rice or beans? Pour in a can of corn, peas, or carrots, and you have a delicious rice dish.

But remember the most important rule: Buy what you eat and eat what you buy. I bet everyone has that odd can of yams, strained pumpkin, or some unusual veggie that never will be eaten. You keep shoving it to the back and to the side of the pantry or burying it behind other items in the cupboard.

Stop right now and do a little exercise. Go to your cupboard, look in the back of it, and see what ancient can you have that no one will ever eat. Were you able to find a can of beets? Leeks? Rutabagas? When you find something you and your family won't ever eat, bag it up and give it to the nearest church food bank. You may never eat it, but there are others out there who might.

Canned Condensed Soup

Whoever invented cream of mushroom soup invented an entire recipe book of meals. Chicken noodle soup is also great to have when folks are feeling sick. And tomato soup—with grilled cheese sandwiches—is a staple when it is snowing. There are vegetable soups, clam chowder, minestrone, corn chowder, and the list goes on and on. One can never have enough soup on hand. But, the one that you need to get is cream of mushroom soup, and lots of it.

Finally…Condiments

Ketchup, mustard, relish, salad dressings, barbecue sauce, Worcestershire sauce, Louisiana hot sauce, soy sauce, teriyaki sauce…you get the idea. The world is a better place because of sauces. Rice, beans, and lentils get really old; that is when sauces come to the rescue. These items tend to be forgotten. But, the wonderful thing is that these items are made to last. Buy twelve of each and you will have enough to last years.

Other sauces you want to remember are spaghetti sauce, tomato sauce, Alfredo sauce, sloppy Joe/hot dog sauce—any sauce that can spice up a meal. Also pick up brown and white gravy mixes; beef, pork, and chicken gravy mixes; soup mixes; beef, chicken, and shrimp bullion; and stew mixes—they are all so convenient. And don't forget the king of mixes: onion soup mix.

If you have a good supply of food and water, you will be able to weather pretty much any storm that may come your way. Make a shopping list to get you started on your food preps, go out and purchase the items, then store them. Every time you go to the grocery store, pick up a few more cans of this or that—an extra bag of sugar, salt, or flour, for example. Always make sure you purchase something that you can add to your food pantry. If you do this, it will not take very long to build a good three- to six-month-supply of food. Once you have your food stores in place, next you need to think about how you will protect them.

chapter five

HOME DEFENSE
Getting a Gun

This is a very touchy subject with many Christians. Many people have had heated conversations about the need to protect yourself and use deadly force if needed. I have already covered what Scripture says, as well as the fact that Christ Himself commanded us to sell our cloaks so that we can purchase a sword.

Now I want to talk about the many different options one has regarding guns. Let me start with what seems the hardest issue—and I do not want to sound sexist, but it is women and guns.

Here is an email I received from a woman:

Hi, Ray:

I am a single woman. I appreciate all the info on your website. My question is: If I buy a gun for personal safety and hunting I'll have to register it and, when the government outlaws guns, I'll have to relinquish it. Wouldn't it be better to buy a small bow and arrow for hunting food and a stun gun for protection? Perhaps you can point me to a discussion of this issue on your web site. God bless you, M

This was a very good question from a concerned woman. There are several things she needs to consider. First, she needs to find out whether she is able to get a carry-and-conceal handgun license where she lives. If she can, that is the route I would go first.

I always say that for personal and home protection, you need to get a handgun. But on top of that, go and get your C&C as well, so that you can always carry it. The nice thing about being a woman and having your C&C is that you can carry a pretty nice weapon in your purse and you won't have a "gun signature" under your clothes.

So I would advise this writer to get a handgun first. (I'll discuss more on the specifics of that topic later in the book.)

Next, I want to address the confiscation/relinquishment issue. Many people are concerned about having the "powers that be" going house to house to confiscate their personal weapons. This took place in New Orleans during the aftermath of Hurricane Katrina. Law-abiding citizens had to give up their weapons—their only means of protecting themselves—due to martial law. My mindset is that if anyone wants to take my guns, he will have to pry them from my cold, dead fingers. The FBI estimates that there are more than 200 million privately owned firearms in the United States. If you add those owned by the military, law enforcement agencies, and museums, there is probably about one gun per person in the country. Now, if you want to get a rough idea of how many guns are out there, just look at how many people you see, then multiply by a factor of estimated ownership. The last best guess was about 350 million–500 million guns out there. That would easily be one weapon for every man, woman, and child living in the U.S. alone.

Don't forget that the average gun enthusiast owns several firearms, including pistols, shotguns, and rifles of all makes and models. It is often estimated that about one in four people own some type of firearm, and the average number of firearms in the home is approximately four guns each. That is a lot of guns to try to take from the American public.

Who in his or her right mind would try to disarm the entire American public? No one could, and no one in his or her right mind would even attempt it.

So…are we going to lose our guns? As much as the "conspiracy folks" want everyone to believe that, I don't believe it is going to happen. Yes, there are cases such as New Orleans and such, but on a nationwide scale, the U.S. government does not have the resources to take all the weapons from every American.

With that said, I recommend that people start buying ammo now because what "they" (the U.S. government) will do is put a serious curb on the purchasing of ammo.

The following article appeared in the *Latin American Herald Tribune* in Venezuela in September 2009:

Venezuela Attempts Gun Control by Limiting Bullets

CARACAS—Legislators at the National Assembly are set to take what appears to be a rather unorthodox approach to law and order in a society notoriously renowned for gun-slinging and one of the highest per capita murder rates on the planet.

The defense committee at the legislature has been looking at a proposed reform of the seventy-year-old Arms and Explosives Law, which apparently has yet to be brought into line with the Bolivarian Constitution adopted by referendum at President Hugo Chávez's behest in late 1999.[17]

We can see that if the government tries to control the guns, it will via the ammunition. So, buy lots of ammo now. Even if you do not own a weapon but are thinking about it, get the ammo now. Consider it a wise investment.

Back to what weapon the email writer should purchase. I am of the opinion that a person's first weapon should be a handgun. This is a home-protection and self-protection weapon. Based on her message, I believe this writer might have been thinking of some sort of rifle, shotgun, or carbine. If you are thinking about a long gun, my choice would be a shotgun.

For home and hunting, the shotgun is a great way to go. I like a "pump" shotgun. There is just something about hearing that *click-clack* of pumping a round in the chamber. Believe me, the "bad guys" know that sound, too, and will "get out of Dodge" quickly when they hear it, because they know that buckshot with their name written on it is coming next.

A shotgun can also be used to hunt. A whole mix of ammo is available for the shotgun, so users can vary the loads. Assuming you can carry at least five rounds of ammunition in the tube, you can make your first round bird shot for close range. It usually will not blast through walls (and if it does, it quickly loses velocity). Second, you can put in a couple of .00 buckshot, followed by a couple of slugs.

Here is my reasoning. First, the "bad guy" is going to be at close range: the bird shot will take him out. The second "bad guy" is going to be a bit farther away: buckshot will take that person out, too. If there is a third person, you have another round of .00 buckshot. Then, if you have a "bad guy" driving the car who is going to fire upon you while you are outside of your front or back door, you have some slugs that will go some distance and do a lot of damage. These will go through walls and if the attacker happens to be hiding behind a car door, you can possibly still get him with the slug.

"Get Started" Gun Recommendations

Hi-Point C-9

My handgun choice, especially if money is a real issue, is the Hi-Point Compact C-9. This shoots a 9 mm, which is a round that I love. This weapon, as of this writing, runs around $165, and has received great reviews. "Gun snobs" out there may not like it, but it is American made and has a lifetime warranty—no questions asked. If something goes wrong, you can send it back to the company for repair or replacement. Hi-Point also makes 380 ACP and 45 ACP versions, but I like the 9 mm because it is compact and good for C&C even though it is a little on the heavy side. Necessity drives determination. You can use the C-9 for C&C and home protection. The grip is also small and fits nicely into a woman's hand.

I am also a big fan of the Walther P22. This is also a great weapon for C&C because it is small, sturdy, and has a weaver rail—a rail built onto the weapon that allows you to mount a laser sight or flashlight.

I consider the Walther P22 as more of a personal C&C weapon than a home-protection weapon. Load up some CCI Stinger .22 ammo, and this is a pretty hot little firearm. Now, it does not have stopping power, but you can become very proficient and train yourself to put all ten rounds into the center mass of the person in a second or two. I don't think many folks will get back up after ten rounds. If they are high on PCP or something, that is a different matter, but the average person will go down. Get extra magazines and carry those with you as well.

Now for shotguns, I like the Mossberg 500 series. The Mossberg 500 is a great all-around shotgun. The turkey version comes with a vented barrel to prevent "barrel rise" with an adjustable choke. It is tapped out so you can put on a scope. This is great for general hunting, and when you're in the home-protection mode, you can put a slug barrel on it for less than one hundred dollars.

The great thing about the 500 is that there are a lot of third-party accessories you can purchase to modify it, including a butt cuff shell holder, a folding stock, a bandoleer strap that holds twenty rounds, and front-end flash lights. These generally run about $250–$350.

Finally, something to think about regarding a shotgun is the "legislative protection." If you are really worried about your weapons being confiscated, the shotgun is regarded by legislators as a sporting arm, and is usually the last type of weapon to be banned or legislated against. This is not always the case, but even in cities like Chicago, it is legal to own a shotgun, whereas handguns and large-capacity magazines are completely banned. This may be extremely helpful for the urban survivalist.

Why Own a Weapon

Craigslist Diamond Ring Ad Leads to Father's Murder in Home Invasion

TACOMA, Wash. (CBS/AP) Four suspects are charged in a fatal home-invasion robbery linked to a Craig's List ad, according to Washington State officials. James Sanders, of the Pierce County community of Edgewood, Wash., was fatally shot on April 28 trying to defend his home from robbers who showed up on the pretext of purchasing a diamond ring he had advertised on the online classified site.

Sanders' wife, Charlene, told reporters last week how the people who pretended to be interested in buying a ring, robbed and beat her family and shot her husband.

"I had a gun to the back of my head with a countdown—three, two—and I'm just screaming and my kids are standing there, and I'm saying, please, God, don't let them kill me, don't let them kill my kids," she said.

She said her husband was shot trying to protect her 14-year-old son who was being pistol-whipped. James Sanders died in his wife's arms.

"I just kept saying 'honey please stay with me, stay with me, stay with us, don't go, don't go,' and he was just barely gasping for air," she said. "They took the love of my live."[18]

Earlier in the book, I talked about how this nation is already in the throes of a financial crisis. The crime rate is also increasing—

and crime is becoming more violent. This article about the Craigslist murder is an example of what I mean regarding people not understanding how things are changing. Not only are many of us students of Bible prophecy, we are watchmen on the wall.

Scripture tells us that in the last days, man's natural affection will "wax worse and worse" (2 Timothy 3:13). That is exactly what we are seeing today. We need to be more alert to our environment. We can't afford to be naive about our surroundings any longer. This also screams as to why we need weapons to protect our families and homes.

What Should Have Happened

First point: James Sanders should have had a firearm at the ready, locked and loaded, while answering the door. Looking through the peephole and giving instructions to the youth, he should have only let one person inside, asking the others to wait at a safe distance even before he opened the door.

If the intruders had refused, he should not have opened the door. He should have called the police—all the while having a firearm at the ready. He should have had the entire family retreat to a safe room, where he could better defend himself. (Having a safe room in the house where you can call the entire family to gather is a very good idea in these days and times. This room needs to have communication, food, water, ammo, extra weapons, and a means to secure the door to prevent intruders from entering. In most cases, this will be the master bedroom. Having an attached bathroom that has tiling on the walls is a plus. You can have your wife and kids get into the tile-lined shower or tub and take cover while you deal with the thugs trying to endanger your life and the lives of your family members.)

If I had let in one of the youths, I would have had a firearm within inches, and would have fired at the first sign of life-threatening danger to me or my family. Letting four youths into my home to look at a diamond ring should have also been a signal of possible danger, but the homeowner let his guard down because he was in his own home. This is very poor situation awareness.

The best scenario would have been for the seller to have met the buyer in a very public place like Starbucks or McDonald's. The seller should ask for a description of the buyer's vehicle and a description of the buyer himself without telling the buyer what he, the seller, looks like or what he drives.

As mentioned earlier, I also endorse having a carry-and-conceal license if allowed. This way, the seller would have been able to keep his family and home out of danger, as well as protect himself by having a firearm ready.

The seller should sit by a window near the counter so he can see the buyer's vehicle or the best possible view of the parking area. This way, the seller can see how many people are occupying the vehicle. The buyer does not know who the seller is or what the seller looks like, so the seller could blend in with the crowd if he suspects foul play.

Four youths in a vehicle should cause suspicion, and the seller should get up and walk out as the "buyer" is walking in. The seller would never be noticed; he could be in his vehicle and out of the area before the buyer puts two and two together.

This is how situations like this should be handled when selling something of value through Craigslist or classified ads. The world is changing before our eyes, and most people are not real-izing it. They still believe that we live in the days of *Leave it to Beaver*. Crime is on the rise, and it will only get worse. The sad thing about the situation in the news article is that the man of the house allowed himself and his family to become victims. He paid the ultimate price for that grievous mistake. My prayers are with the family, and I pray that these predators are given the death sentence for their heinous crime they committed.

My Handgun Recommendations

GLOCK 19
THE 9x19 WORKHORSE

I want to introduce to you a new survival rule. It is called, "The three is two, the two is one, the one is zero" rule. This rule basically means that you always need to have forms of backup. If you only have one handgun and it becomes damaged, taken, or dropped, you have no hand-gun, and this is not a good position to be in. This is why I recommend getting at least two handguns—one primary and one secondary. One can be your carry-and-conceal weapon, and the other can be your home-defense weapon.

I also recommend that you "standardize" your handguns. By this, I mean that all your handguns use the same round and are also made by the same company, with interchangeable parts.

My handgun of choice is the Glock 19. The world over, this is the number-one handgun carried by more police, military, and conceal-and-carry-licensed individuals. The Glock revolutionized the synthetic handgun industry, and today, most handguns of this type have taken many of the design features Glock created.

The Glock is reasonably priced, and has proven itself over and over again in life-and-death situations, performing even under some of the most strenuous situations.

If you go on www.youtube.com and search for "Glock torture testing," you will see a number of videos of people shooting at the Glock with other weapons, burying it for several years, and dropping it from rooftops, multi-story buildings, and even from an airplane. Still, the Glock continues to fire flawlessly.

Taking into account that the Glock 19 will hold fifteen rounds of 9 mm ammo in the magazine and one in the barrel, for a total of sixteen rounds, you are ready to take on multiple assailants (that is, if your state allows the high-capacity, fifteen-round magazine). In most cases in which one has to implement deadly force, it is under an attack with multiple attackers.

The Glock 19 shoots the 9 x 19 mm ammo, also known as Luger 9 mm. This round is probably the most commonly used in the world. Most police and military use this; for this reason, it is inexpensive as well as always in stock at almost any store that sells handgun ammo. In its field-stripped mode, the Glock 19 has four parts: the upper receiver, the lower receiver, the barrel and barrel retention spring/guide rod, and the magazine.

The big brother to the Glock 19 is the Glock 17, which was the first production pistol Glock made. It got its name from being able to hold seventeen rounds of 9 mm in its magazine. Add one to the chamber and you have eighteen rounds. The Glock 26 is the baby brother to the Glocks 19 and 17. Its barrel is shorter, it weighs less, and it carries ten rounds in the magazine and one in the chamber.

What I like about the Glock is that it is a proven battle weapon. It has only thirty-four parts, and all these are pretty much interchangeable among the three models—the 26, 19, and 17.

Glock 19 9mm with tactical flashlight attached.

Many third-party parts and accessories are available for the 9 mm Glock series. In fact, many people customize their Glocks. For example, you can purchase a magazine extender that will fit over a fifteen-round Glock 19 magazine and use it in the smaller Glock 26. This gives you 5 +1 extra ammo, and also helps fit your hand more comfortably.

Want a little longer barrel? Take the barrel out of a Glock 17 and place it in the Glock 19. You can do the same by putting it on a Glock 26.

The Glocks 17 and 19 have built-in picatinny rails under the barrel so that you can attach a flashlight and/or a laser. The manufacturer also makes a thirty-round magazine that will fit all the Glock 9 mm models.

Finally, you can run your Glock through the dishwasher when it gets really dirty. Although the manufacturer does not recommend doing this, plenty of You Tube videos out there show that it can be done with absolutely no harm to the firearm. Just make sure you do not run it through the "drying" cycle, because that might damage the polymer on the lower receiver.

I own and carry the Glock 19 as well as the Glock 26. Their performance is unmatched, and they are built to take serious abuse and still keep firing. You will not go wrong in owning a Glock 19 or any of the Glock 9 mm series.

Glock 26—Note the shorter barrel and hand grip.

Glock 17—The handgun that started it all. This is a third-generation version. Note the picatinny rails under the barrel that will hold a flashlight or laser.

The ammo that I shoot in my Glock 19 is Winchester Supreme Elite Ammunition 9 mm Luger +P 124 Grain Bonded PDX1 Jacketed Hollow Point. This stuff will stop just about anyone.

The FBI has tested this to see if it will stand up to real-world, life-endangering situations. These jacketed hollow points expand one and a half times, and utilize a nickel-plated brass casing to ensure not only smooth chambering of the round, but also proper case ejection. If or when you need to call upon these rounds, you need them to perform—100 percent of the time. I have shot these at the range to make sure they fire properly in my handgun. I have even mixed these with standard Winchester ball ammo, and my Glock 19 has not jammed once. These are what I choose to carry as my ammo of choice.

At a cost of about nineteen dollars for a box of twenty (and sometimes on sale for less), these are probably carried by your local Wal-Mart. If not, check one of the large hunting or sporting goods stores.

The bottom line is this: I highly recommend that one of the

first things you purchase in your entire preps strategy is a handgun for home defense. Don't just buy it and stick it in a drawer, either. As I have said, I totally support going out and getting your carry-and-conceal license if your state allows. I also highly recommend that you take a pistol fundamentals class, as well as a home defense class. Many of these types of classes are held all over the country. The more confident you are with your handgun, the better off you will be if and when the time comes to defend your life and the lives of your loved ones.

The .22 Rimfire Bullet

I like the .22 rimfire bullet for a survival weapon. Now, I know that I will take a lot of flack, but in reality the .22 rimfire is a great all-purpose round in many situations. The first words coming to your mind may be "stopping power" for self-defense. That is a great point, and one that I agree with, but I am talking about all-around survival, not all-out war.

Most of the things that I am going to shoot are rabbits, birds, snakes (rattlers—and we have a lot where I live), feral dogs and cats, coyotes, chickens, turkeys, and other small livestock. These critters are far more likely to be put within my crosshairs than the two-legged ones.

More Handgun Recommendations

The Ruger Mark III Target is all stainless steel, so it will not easily rust. It features a 5.5-inch bull barrel, which improves accuracy. With this gun, you can shoot a fly off the wall at fifty feet, easily. I like the fact that this also comes with a weaver rail so you can mount an "aim point/red dot" sight—or better yet, a laser sight for total point-and-shoot accuracy. This is a great "ranch gun," especially with all the rattlers we have out here at the Gano Ranch. (Did you know that rattlers are good eating too? They taste a lot like tangy chicken.)

I like the .22s because they are pretty inexpensive, with both the Ruger and the Walther P22 both running around three hundred dollars. That's affordable, and it's easy to save for this amount. If you are going to purchase one, check out a gun show; you will be able to shop around and possibly get one of these at a great price.

Both of these are pretty light weight, considering a 9 mm, a .45, or a .357. Now the Ruger Target is a bit heavier. My wife has no problem shooting the bull barrel Ruger, but she does like her Walther P22 better. It fits her smaller hand a lot better and is more comfortable for her to shoot.

A real great point about the .22 is that ammo is dirt cheap. A box of 550 Federal hollow points runs about fifteen dollars at Wal-Mart. Plus, just about anywhere you go, you can purchase .22s. They are pretty easy to find.

Knowing that ammo is cheap, you can get out there and practice...a lot! You know what they say: "Practice makes perfect." Since .22 ammo is cheap, I can run two hundred to three hundred rounds down range without feeling guilty about wasting money or worrying that I won't be able to find ammo to replace what I use.

The benefit is that I become extremely proficient with a smaller-caliber handgun rather than just becoming "so-so" with, say, a .45 or 9 mm that uses more expensive and possibly hard-to-find ammo. In fact, just to emphasize this point, right now, my Wal-Mart does not have any 9 mm or .45 in stock, but it has at least thirty bricks (550 rounds per box) of the Federal hollow points on the shelf.

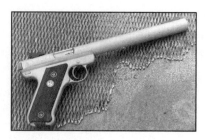

Ruger Amphibian

Other Great Points about the .22

This is a pretty quiet round to shoot compared to a .45 or .357, which sounds like a cannon firing. In addition, the .22 does not have that heavy recoil that many females and kids tend to be concerned about. If you have any sizable property, you can shoot it also and maintain safety. There are many targets with built-in back stops that will handle a .22. So practicing is easy; just make the time to do it.

Now, for all you James Bond wannabes, you may or may not know that many professional assassins use the .22. In fact, go to www.youtube.com and search for "Ruger Amphibian." That is a modified Mark II or III with a fully enclosed suppressor/silencer. The average price for this little beauty is twelve hundred dollars or more. Interestingly, in many states it is actually legal to own one, but you do have to jump through some legal hoops to do it.

Here is a funny story: My friend, a twenty-year Special Forces veteran who now works for a "private company," saw my Ruger and the first thing he tried to do was unscrew the front end to expose the internal section of the suppressor/silencer. I told him it was a standard Mark III bull barrel. He smiled at me and said that a lot of his buddies "at work" carry the Amphibian as a backup. It looked exactly like my Mark III.

Finally, another point about a .22 is that if it gets lost or stolen, replacing it won't set you back several paychecks. Again, we're talking about just a little over three hundred dollars to get a new, in-the-box replacement. Sight it in really quickly, and you are back in action.

So if you are looking for an all-around survival weapon, I like the .22. There are a lot of companies and models to choose from. I am partial to Ruger, made in the good ol' U.S. of A. You can't go wrong with that.

My .22 Rifle of Choice

Ruger 10/22 semiautomatic rifle

If you are looking for a rifle, then it is, hands down, the Ruger 10/22 semiautomatic rifle. It has to be one of the best buys for your money.

The great thing about the Ruger 10/22 is that many third-party companies sell all sorts of add-ons and modifications, including twenty-, thirty-, fifty-, and even hundred-round magazines. The 10/22 is a pretty cool weapon that's fun to modify. At around $300–$350, it is also very affordable—and is a great "varmint" weapon that you can use for shooting cans, hunting, and even self-defense.

All the benefits I mentioned regarding the .22 apply for the Ruger 10/22. The ammo is cheap, so you can practice enough that you become so proficient that you can shoot a fly at one hundred yards or bring home some rabbit for dinner if times get lean.

If you're interested, there is also available a Ruger 10/22 Full Auto Simulator that attaches to your trigger guard and cranks for simulated, full automatic fire. Easy to install, this little gem fits most semi-automatic .22 rifles—BUT it is NOT legal to own, carry, or sell to residents living in California or other liberal states. So if you want one, move to Texas, then you can send all the lead down range you want. All you have to worry about is reloading your magazines.

This little modification costs thirty to forty dollars. In fact, mount a Caldwell lightweight bipod to the front end of your Ruger 10/22, and with the Ruger 10/22 Full Auto Simulator, you can do a lot of damage to that gang of rabbits down range that just keep getting in your cabbage patch. That is a lot of rabbit in the pot and a lot of lead down range.

So this is why one of my weapons of choice in a survival situation is the .22. Everyone can become very proficient with it. Ammo is cheap and readily available. The cost of getting a .22 is really reasonable, and if you are a first-time gun owner, the .22 is a great place to start.

Shooting and hunting are great sports and an American heritage. In today's political climate, we need to be exercising more of our rights and passing on more of our heritage. Because if we don't, we will have neither.

The Shotgun and Reasons You Need One

The shotgun is probably the most versatile firearm that you can own, and I believe that every prepper needs to have at least one in his home armory. I know that some folks out there disagree, but the shotgun is more powerful than a handgun. Here are other reasons I recommend owning a shotgun.

Reason #1—Price

Like it or not, everyone is concerned about money. The good news is that you can go to just about any sporting goods store that offers firearms and find shotguns. They are everywhere, and they are cheaper than the alternatives: an AR-15 or an AK-47. If you have two or three hundred dollars, you can walk into your local sporting goods store, gun shop, or mega store and easily walk out with a shotgun under your arm. Knowing this, you can quickly save the money you need, and within a week or two, you can upgrade your preps plan and add a shotgun to your home armory.

Now I did mention an AR-15 or AK-47, but those cost considerably more and the goal of this book is to get you ramped up with your preps as quickly as possible. Once you are adequately prepped, you can then start expanding.

Reason #2—Different Types of Ammunition

As I mentioned previously, a whole mix of different ammo is available for the shotgun, and you can vary your loads also. Assuming you can carry at least five rounds of ammunition in the tube, you can make your first round birdshot for close range. They will not blast through walls, but if you happen to be standing close enough when you shoot that they do penetrate a wall, they lose velocity really quickly. Second, you can put a couple of rounds of .00 buckshot, followed by a couple of rounds of 12-gauge slugs.

Here is a home-defense scenario:

It is late at night and you hear a noise in your home. You then hear multiple voices coming from the front of the house. Sitting next to your bed is your trusty Mossberg 500, and you have prepared just for this type of situation.

You know your home, so you use the corners and concealment to your advantage. You see the first bad guy, and he has got a gun sticking out of the front of his pants. He is at a close range, and your first round in your shotgun is birdshot. At this range, it will cut him to ribbons and take him out.

You fire, and bad guy number one goes down.

The second bad guy you see is coming towards you. He is to be a bit farther away, but that is OK; your second round in the stack is buckshot, and it will take out that person before he reaches you. You do not know if there is another bad guy, but you have another round of .00 buck ready and waiting.

All of a sudden, bullets are coming through the front window. Another guy was driving the car. You have that buckshot chambered already, so you fire, shattering the car windows. But that is not all: You have some slugs that will go some distance in the stack, and they do a lot more damage.

Bad guy number three took up a position outside the car, and he is now shooting blindly through the blown-out car windows. He is using the old "spray-and-pray" method, and is not even coming close to you. You chamber the slug, knowing these will go through walls as well as car doors. *BLAM! CLICK-CLACK! BLAM!* You send two slugs down range, and both are right on target. It is quiet. Taking more buckshot from your rifle butt carrier, you load more into your shotgun. You have eliminated the bad guys. Practicing this exercise over and over again has paid off; you and your family are safe, and the bad guys are finished.

Yes this is kind of glorified, but it is a good example of stacking different rounds in your shotgun in anticipation of the need. Birdshot is good for small game or for close-quarter, indoor defense. Upland game rounds, with larger BBs, pack a meaner punch. And .00 buckshot is like sending eight rounds of 9 mm down range. Then the slug, with one big, 50 mm hunk of lead, is like a cannonball. There are also many different types of rounds in between these. The shotgun even has the capability of shooting rounds that contain nonlethal bean bags, rubber bullets, or even small nets that deploy when they exit the shotgun bore. So the variety of shotgun rounds is pretty extensive, and there is probably a round to meet every need.

Reason #3—Power and Performance

The power the shotgun delivers beats a handgun, hands down. Whereas the handgun has maneuverability and high capacity, the shotgun delivers a deadly volley of BBs, buckshot and slugs. These have been the weapon of choice for law enforcement. In fact, the term "riding shotgun" comes from the days when a stagecoach driver was accompanied by a person acting as security, who carried a sawed-off, double-barrel shotgun.

Shotguns were used during the bloody trench warfare of World War I. The Allies brutalized the Germans so badly with the shotgun that the Germans protested their use and threatened to instantly execute any troops found in possession of them. During Vietnam, shotguns were used by the tunnel rats who went deep into the Vietcong tunnels clearing out the enemy. Fast forward to today, and our military boys stationed in Iraq have used the shotgun effectively to clear out structures during building-to-building searches seeking out the enemy.

Reason #4—Easy to Maintain

Most shotguns are very easy to maintain. In fact, breaking down a pump shotgun is easy, and with a little practice you can even change out to a different barrel, depending on the situation. There are plenty of different cleaning solvents and oils that you can use, and most, if not all, can be used on the common shotgun with no problem. In fact, if things get bad, you can even use a cut-up t-shirt soaked with gasoline or diesel fuel and wrapped over the end of a bamboo pole to get your shotgun clean. It isn't rocket science, and the shotgun is designed to keep things simple.

Reason #5—Different Roles a Shotgun Can Play

The basic pump shotgun can play a vast array of different roles. For example, you can pull your long hunting barrel off and put on the shorter, home-defense barrel and you have converted your shotgun from a recreation tool to a "get-the-bad-guys" defensive weapon. Or, you can swap out the common wooden stock and replace it with a camo or flat, black, nylon stock and front forearm. You can even get dual pistol grips, one for the trigger and one for the forearm, to have a tactical weapon at the ready. There are flashlights, lasers, twenty-round bandoleer slings, scopes, red dot sights, and even holographic heads-up sights for your shotgun. You can get a short barrel or a long barrel, or even one that is between those two sizes. Use folding stocks, collapsible stocks, or even no stocks, using a single pistol grip. If you can think it up, the odds are that it's available for the shotgun, which is capable of wearing many different hats effectively.

Reason #6—Protected by the Law

Even with all the different roles the shotgun can play, it is still seen as a sporting arm by legislators, and because of this, it will be the last type of weapon to be banned or have legislation drawn against it. You can even own a shotgun in some of the most anti-gun havens in the U.S. In New York City they are legal to own, and even in Chicago—where handguns have been completely banned—it's legal to own a shotgun. This in and of itself is something that the modern-day prepper needs to remember, and it's why I say that everyone needs to have at least one shotgun in the home armory.

Choosing a Shotgun

Now let's talk about the type of shotgun that is good for you.

Choosing the Gauge

The gauge is the size of the diameter of the barrel, as measured from the rear of the weapon. The gauge determines the size round the shotgun can fire. There are different gauges of shot guns, starting with the smallest, .410, then moving up to .20, then moving up again to the most popular gauge, .12.

Other, big-bore gauges such as .10 and .8 are available, but they are not very common, and are more expensive.

The 410 Shotgun

The .410 is a small-bore round, about half the diameter of a dime or a little bigger than the diameter of a No. 2 pencil. This type of shotgun is usually a boy's first. Commonly, it is a breach break—meaning it breaks open at the breach, or where the stock of the rifle and the shotgun barrel meet. You have to feed one round per shot into this type of shotgun. These are good for small game and dove, as well as for taking care of vermin like rats, snakes, and mice. They have very little kick at all. I do not recommend them to be used in a home-defense role because they really do not have the size or enough firepower (but they can be used as a backup weapon if a firefight ensues.)

Rounds include snake shot, birdshot, upland game, buckshot (three to four balls), and slug, with other sizes in between. This is a good weapon for a teenage boy or girl learning to hunt and shoot.

The 20-Gauge Shotgun

Most people get a 12-gauge shotgun, but once they really start shooting it, their shoulders wish they would have taken a 20 gauge. For a home-defense weapon that everyone in the family can use, I recommend a 20 gauge. It has enough firepower to it to be effective, but not quite the kick that a 12 gauge has. This is a very woman- and teenager-friendly shotgun. Teaching everyone how to use a 20 gauge is a very good home-defense solution. One cannot always say that the man of the house will be within arm's reach of the shotgun. Having one that both the wife and kids can effectively use is a very smart tactical solution. This is why I like the 20 gauge for an all-around, general, home-defense shotgun as well as a good hunting weapon.

The 12-Gauge Shotgun

For most preppers out there, the hands-down standard for the shotgun is going to be a 12-gauge pump. As discussed earlier, you can pick one up just about anywhere that sells firearms.

There are also the semi-automatic shotguns, which are great; however, with more working parts, they have more of a chance that something will go wrong. And you can't just break down a semi-auto shotgun and do a quick repair on it, whereas with a pump you can usually pull it apart, find the problem, and get back in the action.

Pump shotguns are pretty inexpensive, but semi-auto shotguns cost three to four times more than pumps. Sure, some models are less expensive, but the inexpensive ones tend to jam up and break—always at the worst possible moment. Are you willing to gamble your life and the lives of your family members on a cheap, semi-auto shotgun?

Then there is the issue of parts. It takes more parts to cycle that semi-auto than there are parts in the standard pump shotgun. These parts will wear out and eventually break—again, usually at the worst possible time. There is also the issue of bad feeds and finicky ammo, whereas a pump shotgun will "eat" almost any round you put in the magazine. Semi-autos have been known not to like all rounds or sizes, which results in the weapon jamming. If a pump jams up, it is relatively easy to clear; but if a semi-auto jams up, you are basically out of the fight until you can clear that jam.

My Choices of Shotgun

When it comes right down to it, there really are only two choices: The Mossberg 500 and the Remington 870.

Mossberg 500

Personally, I like the Mossberg 500; in fact, I own a Mossberg 500 Tactical Turkey Series pump shotgun. But when you butt up weapon to weapon, both models are excellent and dependable shotguns. These two are probably the most famous and the most widely owned shotguns. They are both affordable, and you can find them at almost any sporting goods store, Wal-Mart or other mega mart, or gun shop. Both Mossberg and Remington make different varieties of the individual shotgun.

Mossberg 500 Tactical Turkey Series pump shotgun

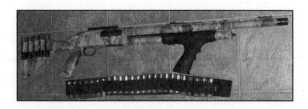

The Mossberg 500 has a front and rear pistol grip and a modified butt that holds six extra rounds. The Tactical Turkey is already drilled for a scope, but a weaver rail has been added to the top so that a red dot or a holographic rear sight can be used.

The Remington 870 Sportsman Synthetic

As I have said, it is a toss-up between the Mossberg 500 and the Remington 870. They are both fine weapons and the Mossberg wins by just a hair.

When I was going to purchase my shotgun, I was using an older gun for a trade. I had limited amount of cash, and had my eye on a Remington 870 ShurShot Super Turkey. I really liked the feel of this weapon, with its Monte Carlo stock and built-in pistol grip. But it was slightly out of my price range.

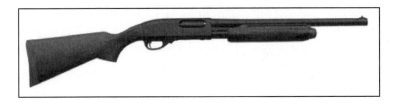

Remington 870

Both of these shotguns come in 12-gauge and 20-gauge. Head down to your local gun shop and feel both of them. Look at all their features, as well as the third-party add-ons.

In fact, regarding third party add-ons: The Mossberg 500 has a few advantages over the Remington 870 besides the price. It was that ability to have the opportunity to add a few more modifications that finally won me over to the Mossberg 500.

But either of these will fit the bill and will serve you for a long time to come.

Other Weapons of Honorable Mention

There are so many different handguns, shotguns, rifles, and carbines that I can't mention every single one, but I do want to mention a few that are worth consideration.

1911 .45 ACP

The 1911 .45 ACP was the standard for the U.S. Army until about twenty years ago, when it switched over to the Beretta 92 9 mm. The 1911 was invented in—you guessed it—1911 by Sam Colt of Colt Manufacturing Co. Many different companies now produce a version of the 1911, and all have pretty much the same build and make-up. Other companies worth mentioning are Kimber, Springfield Armory, and Smith & Wesson, to name a few. You can depend on almost any well-known company that makes the 1911.

Point to consider: I used to own a 1911, but I found that getting .45 ACP ammunition was very difficult. Many times, Wal-Mart—as well as other stores—would be completely out of it. When the store wasn't out of it, I would purchase at least fifty or one hundred rounds just so I would have some on hand. This is one of the main reasons I switched over to the 9 mm and chose the Glock 19. A .45 ACP is also more expensive. Winchester ammo costs almost twice as much as the Federal. In fact most .45 ACP costs more than 9 mm ammunition. This tends to be the average when it comes to cost comparisons between 9 mm and .45 ACP.

The Colt Python .357 Magnum

The official Colt historian, R. L. Wilson, described the Colt Python as "the Rolls-Royce of Colt revolvers," and firearms historian Ian V. Hogg referred to it as the "best revolver in the world." But many people remember the Colt .357 from the *Dirty Harry* movies starring Clint Eastwood.

These are the "hand cannons" of modern times. Then along came the .44 Magnum. Dirty Harry upgraded his firearm and the line, "Go ahead punk, make my day," while he held his .44 Magnum three inches from the guy's nose.

The .357 Mag is a good weapon, but it is a revolver, which means it only takes six rounds and then needs to be reloaded. Another problem with the Colt Python is that after you own and shoot it for a while, it can get out of time, meaning that the cylinder does not move in sequence with the hammer being drawn back and released. The result of this is a round not firing. Many police carried the .357 Magnum until this problem was discovered. Colt was able to remedy the problem, but it never bounced back as the "Rolls Royce of revolvers."

This is a good handgun to own—and it could be used for home defense—but there is too much power in the weapon, and the bullets easily go through walls. Even shooting a hollow point, the rounds still exit and put whatever is behind the target in danger.

What the Colt .357 Mag has become is an excellent hog-hunting gun for those who like to hunt wild boar with a handgun. The .357 Magnum bullet will drop a hog right away.

The Taurus .38 Ultralite Revolver

"Ultra-fast, Ultra-reliable, Ultra-lightweight." That is how Taurus markets its ultra-light .38 Special revolver. The .38 Special was once the weapon of choice with many in law enforcement nationwide. The snub-nose, one-inch barrel was the ultimate in carry-and-conceal handguns. Today, these are making a popular comeback for C&C because they are being made from special alloy metals that greatly reduce the weight. They are becoming very popular with women who have their C&C license. In fact, some companies are even making the frames in pink to attract more female purchases.

These are good weapons, and can be used for home defense. Using a +P hollow point, you can take down the bad guys. The negative, in my opinion, is that it only holds six rounds; learning to reload quickly and effectively takes a lot of practice. In the time it takes to reload, the bad guys can have the jump on you, and they can win. This is why I like weapons with a high-capacity magazine like the Glock 19, which holds fifteen in the mag and one in the chamber, totaling sixteen rounds. The Glock 17, one step up from the 19, holds seventeen in the mag and one in the chamber, with a total of eighteen rounds. Couple this with another fifteen- to seventeen-round magazine waiting, and that is at least thirty rounds you can send down range if needed.

On the plus side, many people like having the .38 as a backup weapon. There is no racking the slide to the rear, or anything like that. You just pull the trigger and it fires. This in and of itself makes for a pretty safe weapon.

Semi-Automatic Paramilitary Rifles

You are probably wondering why it took me so long to get to these types of weapons. The primary reason is that, considering the overall cost of prepping, I consider the semi-automatic rifle a luxury when much more gear, supplies, and other things need to be acquired first.

The two weapons of choice in this category are the AR-15 and the AK-47. Sure, there are others, but these are the most common. The availability of parts, ammo, and third-party accessories make these two weapons probably the most widely used in the world.

But I want to stress that it is important to have at least 75 percent of the rest of your preps in place before allocating the money to purchase one of these weapons. The AR-15 costs (just for a down-to-basic, old-fashioned model) around $875—and that is a bare-bones rifle. The price goes up from there. One with fancy weaver rails, a front-end grip, a heavy-duty, chrome-plated barrel, and flip-up sights, etc., can cost around eleven hundred dollars and up.

You can get a run-of-the-mill Romanian AK-47 clone off the Internet starting at around $450, but you need to have it shipped to someone with a Federal Firearms License. In the stores here in Texas, they are running about six hundred dollars. Magazines holding thirty rounds for the AK-47 cost around ten dollars, and the price is about the same for an AR-15 magazine. The older Colt metal mags are a little more costly.

AR-15

About the AR -15

The AR-15 was created by Eugene Stoner when he worked for ArmaLite; that is how we get the "AR" in the name of this weapon. ArmaLite sold the rights for the AR-15 to Colt about fifty years ago. Today, AR-15s are manufactured by quite a few companies in every shape and design you can think of.

The AR-15 is a gas-operated, semi-automatic rifle chambered for .223 and/or 5.56. This means that the gas from the explosion that takes place at the rear of the weapon is used to cycle the weapon. The AR-15 will shoot the round, eject the spent casing, pick up another round, load it into the chamber, cock the hammer, and fire the round. All of this takes place almost as fast as the blink of an eye.

ArmaLite designed the weapon to be built using nylon, plastic, and aluminum. This reduced its weight while also maintaining rigidity. It shoots a relatively small-caliber round that is just a hair's breadth bigger than a run-of-the-mill .22.

What makes the .223 different is that it has a very large amount of gunpowder behind that small .22 round, shooting it at a very high velocity. Another aspect of the round is that when it is shot, due to the twist of the barrel, it causes the round to "tumble" end over end. When it hits, this tumbling effect makes the round bounce all over.

It is not uncommon to hear that the round, when entering a human body, enters through the shoulder and exits through the thigh or some sort of odd entry and exit. Very rarely does the .223 enter and leave via a straight trajectory. When it hits you, the bullet bounces around your insides like a ball being played in a pinball machine. It goes in, but one never knows where it will exit.

AR-15 vs. M-16

It was the M-16 that our American fighting men used from the early 1960s until now. Today, they use what is called an M-4, but this is built off of the M-16/AR-15 model. It has been highly modified and refined to meet the needs of the modern military fighting man in today's service. What makes the AR-15 different from the M-16 is that the AR-15 is capable of SAFE or SEMI-auto fire only, and the M-16 has SAFE, SEMI-auto, and FULL. In other words, the M-16 is a fully automatic machine gun, able to empty a full, thirty-round magazine in just a couple of seconds.

Other features also make the AR-15 and the M-16 different. For example, they have different triggers, disconnecters, selectors, bolt carriers, and hammers. I say this because, despite the many urban legends, how-to books, and web pages out there, it is not all that easy to convert an AR-15 into an M-16. One needs good precision drills, presses, and such—items the average prepper does not usually have.

I am a big fan of the AR-15. It is easy to use and maintain, and finding ammo is pretty easy. If you are in the position to get an AR-15, I highly recommend it, but not at the expense of forsaking your other preps.

AK-47

The AK-47

Russian Mikhail Kalashnikov designed the AK-47 because his homeland had been invaded by an enemy with superior weapons. What drove him to design it was his personal witnessing of his fellow soldiers and civilians being gunned down in World War II by the Nazis. He determined that would never happen again. He began to work on the design in 1944 and presented the weapon to the military in 1946. After running the weapon through its paces, the *Avtomat Kalashnikova*, commonly known as the AK, was born in 1947—thus the name of the AK-47.

The AK-47 has to be seen as one of the most successful weapons of all times, and is used all over the world. In the movie *Heartbreak Ridge*, Clint Eastwood's character made this memorable quote: "This is the AK-47 assault rifle, the preferred weapon of your enemy; and it makes a distinctive sound when fired at you, so remember it."

He then shot above the heads of his troops so that they would have that sound drilled into their heads.

When I was with the 82nd Airborne, we trained and became experts with the M-16 as well as with the AK-47. That is because it was our mission to be dropped behind enemy lines, disrupt supply, and ambush the enemy. Although we carried the M-16, we would not be able to be resupplied with ammo once we ran out. Since the AK-47 was used by both the Vietcong and the Mujahideen against the Soviet Union in Afghanistan, we could carry on our mission with their weapons and ammo once our supply was gone.

The AK-47 fires the 7.62 x 39 mm cartridge. To put it in layman's terms, the casing is about the same size as an M-16, but it has the bullet of a .308 hunting rifle. Although the bullet does not have the long-distance range, it does pack a punch due to the large, .308 projectile.

Customized AK-47 with tactical flashlight, red dot scope, and forward hand grip—all mounted on weaver rails on the front, with collapsible stock on the rear.

Many variants of the weapon have been produced since 1947. The following is from Wikipedia's page about the AK-47:

- **AK-47 1948–51, 7.62 x 39 mm**—The very earliest models, with the Type 1 stamped sheet metal receiver, are now very rare.
- **AK-47 1952, 7.62 x 39 mm**—Has a milled receiver and wooden butt-stock and hand-guard. Barrel and chamber are chrome plated to resist corrosion. Rifle weight is 4.2 kg (9.3 lb).

- **AKS-47**—Featured a downward-folding metal stock similar to that of the German MP40, for use in the restricted space in the BMP infantry combat vehicle, as well as by paratroops.
- **RPK, 7.62 x 39 mm**—Hand-held machine gun version with longer barrel and bipod.
- **AKM, 7.62 x 39 mm**—A simplified, lighter version of the AK-47; Type 4 receiver is made from stamped and riveted sheet metal (see schematic above). A slanted muzzle device was added to counter climb in automatic fire. Rifle weight is 3.1 kg (6.8 lb.) due to the lighter receiver. This is the most ubiquitous variant of the AK-47.
- **AKMS, 7.62 x 39 mm**—Folding-stock version of the AKM intended for airborne troops. Stock may be either side- or under-folding.
- AK-74 series, 5.45 x 39 mm
- AK-101/AK-102 series
- AK-103/AK-104 series
- AK-107/AK-108 series
- AK-200 series
- **Saiga semi-automatic rifle**—AK variant for hunting and civilian use. Built on AK receiver with hunting style stock and hand guard in 223/5.56, 7.62 x 39, 5.45 x 39, 308WIN.
- **Saiga semi-automatic shotgun**—AK variant for hunting and civilian use. Built on AK receiver with hunting style stock and hand guard in 12-gauge, 20-gauge, and .410-bore.[19]

I like the AK-47 just as much as I like the AR-15. In fact, there are points to the AK-47 that I like even better than the AR-15. For example you can take a hand full of dirt, put it in the upper receiver of the AK-47, and the weapon will still shoot without jamming up. Do that with an AR-15, and not a single round will come out.

The only thing that I do not like about the AK-47 is that its ammo can be difficult to find. However, when you do find it, especially at a gun show, it is relatively inexpensive. You can get a case sealed in what looks like a big, old-fashioned sardine can. It has thirty-two boxes of twenty rounds each. The Wolf 7.62 x 39 Military Sealed Tin with 640 rounds costs about $220. That comes up to be approximately $6.85 for a box of twenty. That isn't a bad price, and you can even find it cheaper if you really do some looking on the Internet. The ammo for an AR-15 is about seven or eight dollars for a box of twenty.

Over all, the AR-15 and the AK-47 are excellent investments if you have the need to "reach out and touch somebody." Either one would round out the home armory very nicely.

chapter six

EVERYDAY CARRY AND BECOMING THE GRAY MAN

"Gray man: A man who can blend in to any scene or situation without standing out, hiding his skills and qualities."
—www.urbandictionary.com

Becoming the gray man is an important skill, one you will need in the days to come. You will need to learn how to blend into your environment, look like everyone else, and become the "average-looking Joe."

What makes you different is that you are alert to your surroundings, you suspect everyone who comes within your twenty-foot perimeter, and you are ready to react if the need arises. The real mission is to just be left alone while putting off that "sheep-dog" disposition instead of being one of the sheep.

You are not some weekend warrior or paramilitary nut; you are just like everyone else except that your everyday carry gear probably includes your keys, a cell phone, your wallet, and a wrist watch…as well as a folding, lock-blade knife, a multitool, pepper spray, possibly a flashlight, and if you are C&C licensed, a handgun with an extra-loaded magazine.

If this describes you, you have adapted to the New Normal that we now call America. Crime, looting, blocked roads due to riots, muggings, theft, rape, and murder. These are more commonplace today than the days of yesteryear.

"Then said he unto them, But now, he that hath a purse, let him take it, and likewise his scrip: and he that hath no sword, let him sell his garment, and buy one" (Luke 22:36).

We live in a time when going to the mega mart or the grocery store is an act of bravery, determination, logistics, and security. No longer is it just running to get a gallon of milk and a dozen eggs.

Not that way in your area yet? Just wait.

How to Be the Gray Man

Look around. What are all the guys wearing? (I am focusing on the guys because I am a guy. Ladies, this is for you also; take my examples and adapt them to what you would wear.) Here in the Texas hill country, the majority of men wear some sort of cargo shorts, which go to just above the knee and tend to be a little baggy. Beige, brownish red, or blue jeans tend to be the color of choice.

For a shirt, they wear a common t-shirt that is loose fitting, sometimes with a pocket on the left breast. Or, if they want to dress up a little, they might wear a button-up short sleeve, usually made of some sort of cotton print. I wear a common black, blue, or beige Fruit of the Loom pocket t-shirt or a short-sleeved button-up with a left breast pocket.

Here in Texas, hunting is a big deal and everyone gets in the mode. So when it gets close to hunting season, around the beginning of August, the "real-tree" camo t-shirts become the norm. (It helps that the local Wal-Mart sells these for only six dollars each.)

On their feet, most men wear are ankle socks or rolled-over tube socks under sneakers or some form of work boots. And finally, they wear a common baseball cap and sunglasses.

This is what an "average Joe" looks like in casual dress out on the street, and it is how I usually dress, avoiding loud, logo-based shirts, and usually wearing no jewelry except my wedding ring. I wear nothing that makes me stand out.

If someone asked about you, could they describe you, or would they be describing just about everyone else, the average Joe?

How NOT to Dress

Don't wear bright colors or high fashion—wear nothing that makes you stand out. For example, here in Texas, we have a lot of cowboys walking around—but they are not dressed in the typical cowboy dress. In other words, the cowboys here aren't wearing the long-sleeved shirts with fringes dangling, ten-gallon cowboy hats, or fancy rhinestone pants. Everyone imagines that the average cowboy looks like Roy Rogers or Hopalong Cassidy, but he doesn't. The average cowboy looks just like the person described above, except that he probably wears some sort of work jeans instead of cargo shorts. Come fall and winter here in Texas, we all look like the average "cowboy."

Once in a while, you will see someone wearing a cowboy hat. Straw cowboy hats are acceptable for guys over fifty during the summertime. During the winter, everyone switches from straw to black felt hats. Believe me, if you step out of this mold, you will be noticed, and that is not what you want to do.

If you are a prepper, you do not want to be dressing in some sort of combat BDU pants, army boots, and shirts with para-military sayings like "Death from Above" or pictures that you see at all the gun shows. These shout, "HEY! Look at me! I am a weekend warrior."

Become the Gray Man

Become the average Joe and blend into your surroundings, but walk with a purpose and be alert to what is going on around you. Project a demeanor that tells the wolves, "Leave me alone; I am not one of the sheep. Don't mess with me."

The sheep will not notice you, just like real sheep do not really notice the sheepdog. But the wolves will see you. Wolves are cowards who seek out the weak, frail, and innocent. They do not want to have to work too hard; they want to be in and out, and finish the job.

So while you don't want to be wearing some neon sign blink-ing "GUN...GUN...GUN...KNIFE...KNIFE...KNIFE, with an arrow pointing at you, you do want to be acknowledged as someone who is alert, aware, and not a soft target.

Achieve this is by training yourself. Look like you are some-one who is alive, not like some drained zombie who stares at the ground, shoulders slumped as if he has the weight of the world on his shoulders. Make eye contact and smile at people; greet them and wish them a good day. You don't want to seem like some bodyguard type, either—you know, the guys with the little curly tube sticking out of their ear, wearing dark Ray-Ban glasses and constantly scanning around them, ready to pounce at a moment's notice. That is going overboard.

Out in Public

Mega stores are where America shops; they are also where the wolves hang out for some quick prey. When walking in the parking lot of one of these stores, have a determination to your step. Enter the store, look the greeter in the eye, nod your head, say hello, and smile. Then take a basket, eye the cashier and the customers who are checking out, assess whether anyone seems out of place, then move on for that gallon of milk, that dozen eggs, and a few extra boxes of ammo.

However, if you enter the store, scan the area, and notice someone wearing a trench coat when it is ninety degrees outside, this should raise red flags. If this happens, step up the pace. Move into the store, get out of the general area, and do your shopping.

Everyday Carry—EDC

Everyday Carry, or EDC, is part of being the gray man. You want your EDC kit to be well thought out and light in weight. In essence, you want a few items that will help you in case of the common emergency, as well items that will help you protect yourself if necessary.

My EDC doesn't make me look like I am wearing Batman's utility belt. My clothes do not scream "Hey! It's Mr. Tactical Guy here!"—and I do not have so much gear on that I look like Rambo.

I wear Wrangler brand cargo shorts with cargo pockets on each side as well as a cell-phone pocket that opens above the cargo flap. A right side pocket has a coin pocket deep inside, and, finally, there are left and right rear pockets. I wear a double-thick Justin Boots black leather belt with a common cowboy belt buckle. Your belt needs to be sturdy enough to carry all your gear (if you do not put the items in your pockets), as well as hold up your pants, so you do not want some inexpensive belt from the mega stores. Invest some money in this and you will not be sorry. You would be surprised how heavy a cell phone, a buck knife, and a multitool are when you are carrying them on your hip. A heavy-duty belt also helps distribute the weight of these items more evenly. Once you get used to them, you forget they are even there. (On another note: My belt is also a last-ditch defensive weapon. The buckle weighs a good ten to twelve ounces, makes for a mean bludgeon, and can help keep someone at an arm's distance if needed.)

I developed my EDC by starting out carrying just one item, then adding another, and then another. It took time to get used to carrying the gear, finding a spot to carry it in with easy access, and keeping it from banging around on my leg or chest. Some strategies work better than others. Carry what tools and gear you need, but don't make it obvious that you are a prepper—or you will risk looking like some paramilitary tactical guy.

Look around to see what others in your area are carrying, and adapt to that look. If everyone carries a backpack, carry a backpack. If they carry a messenger bag, then a messenger bag is for you. With either of these options, you can also carry a water bottle, a small first-aid kit, and any other gear that is important to you. Just remember to keep it light; you do not want to turn yourself into a pack mule.

When I am dressed up, I usually wear black jeans, black cowboy boots, a black long-sleeve shirt, and a tie. If I need to dress up more, I wear a beige twill sport coat. This is what the average guy wears here in Texas when he dresses up, so I am still blending in and looking good, too. And in all of this, I can still carry most of my gear.

Head-to-Toe EDC

As I have mentioned, it took me a while to develop my EDC. In fact, every good prepper will always be developing and refining his or her EDC. You may purchase an item, carry it one day, and find out that it is not functional or too heavy; there can be any reason. This is why I always keep my receipts and return items I do not use.

Baseball Cap—Here in Texas, it is almost always hot, and I tend to sweat. My baseball cap serves a dual purpose. First, it helps keep the sun out of my eyes and my head covered. Second, it helps soak up the sweat and keep it from dripping into my eyes.

Sunglasses—Not only do I wear these to keep the sun at bay, but I also wear them for protection and anonymity. My sunglasses are the "mirrored" kind so people cannot tell where I am looking when I am scanning the area. These are shatter resistant and scratch resistant for my protection, just in case I am driving and someone hurls a brick or rock through my window.

Left Breast Pocket

UZI Tactical Defender Pen—This is made of lightweight aircraft aluminum, it conveniently uses any standard pen refill, and also doubles as a "Kubaton" with a writing point that can be used for stabbing, and a pointed top for blows to the temple, under the chin, or in the cheek. It will also break a car window if you need to escape.

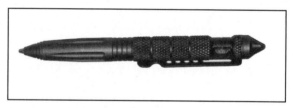

UZI Tactical Defender Pen

Cold Steel Inferno OC Spray Pen—I am a big fan of Cold Steel's Inferno products. In my opinion, these are the best. The primary reason is that they deliver a foam spray rather than a liquid spray, preventing the hazard of liquid blowing back into the operator's face. Check out the company's website at www.coldsteel.com. I also carry a small, flip-open leather ID case that holds my driver's license and bank card.

What Is Inferno?

Inferno is a new pepper spray produced by Cold Steel. What makes it such an effective weapon is that, unlike other sprays that are liquid, Inferno is foam. You can control the pepper spray more effectively than you can the common, liquid type. Once the foam hits the attacker's face, it instantly melts. There are other foam sprays out there, but they do not melt instantly. This enables the attacker to wipe the foam off his or her face, and then possibly use it against you.

Inferno pepper spray, when applied, causes the capillaries of the eye to dilate, resulting in temporary blindness. The black pepper and capsicum (habanero chili extract) cause choking, coughing, and even nausea. The black pepper also immediately induces a sneeze reflex. This action draws the capsicum deep into the nasal cavity, throat, and lungs, instantly debilitating the attacker. The attacker feels like he or she cannot breathe, and becomes incapacitated for quite some time—time enough for you to get away and call the police.

Right Hand, Cell-Phone Cargo Pocket

In my upper-right pants pocket, I usually carry a Leatherman Skeletool CX Multitool. This is not the average multitool.

Here are the specs.

Tools:
- 154 cm stainless-steel, clip-point knife
- Needle-nose pliers
- Regular pliers
- Wire cutters
- Hard-wire cutters
- Large bit driver
- Bottle opener
- Carabiner clip
- Included bits: Phillips #1 and #2; screwdriver $3/16$" and $1/4$"

Features:

- DLC-coated, stainless-steel handles with carbon-fiber handle insert
- Stainless-steel body
- Outside-accessible blade for one-handed opening
- All locking blades and tools
- Removable pocket clip
- DLC coating for scratch and corrosion resistance
- Nylon sheath—sold separately
- Twenty-five-year warranty

Measurements:

- 4 in. | 10 cm (closed)
- 5.0 oz. | 142 g
- 2.6 in. | 6.60 cm (blade length)

The feature I like most about this model is the weight—at only five ounces, it weighs about as much as my pocket knife. The Leatherman Skeletool CX Multitool has the basic tools that, nine times out of ten, are you the only ones you will ever need. I mean, how often do you really use the wine bottle opener on a Swiss army knife? I know that I don't! So why carry that extra weight around when you don't have to? This multitool, in my opinion, is the best one out there.

Right-Hand Pants Pocket

I carry one of two knives, depending on the situation, what I am wearing, and where I am going.

5.11 Tactical Folding Lock-Blade Knife—This is my most prized possession. One of my Prophezine subscribers gave this to me, and I could never replace it if it I ever lose or break it. I use this as a utility knife for cutting just about everything. I keep it razor sharp, and can deploy it in less than a second. The blade is three and one-half inches long, and is legal to carry in most states. This leaves my right-hand side cargo pocket free to carry other items as needed. I do not carry anything in my right-hand rear pocket.

Cold Steel Voyager Large Lock-Blade Knife—The second knife that I carry in my right hand, and this is my right-hand knife of choice, is a Cold Steel Lg Voyager with a serrated blade. The older model of this knife, the one that I own, has been discontinued, but as of this writing, I learned that Cold Steel is reintroducing a better and more ergonomic model of the Voyager. I like to use this as my primary knife because the Voyager Lg series offers light-ning-quick, one-handed opening. This is done by either using the "thumb tab" or by using a flick of the wrist, with the knife being deployed using the inertia of taking it out of the pocket. This is a skill that must be practiced so that you can do this even under stress. I like the Cold Steel Voyager because you can "flick" it open in many different positions, as well as with different hand and arm movements. The blade is five inches long; the handle is approximately six inches long. Overall, the knife comes in at eleven inches in total length. This is important, because this extra eleven inches of reach can make a critical difference if you're being attacked. The size and length of this knife also make a statement: People will think twice when you deploy a knife like this.

Left-Hand Cell Phone Cargo Pocket

Cold Steel Spartan Folding Lock Blade Knife—This is what I call my "battle knife." I do not use it for anything else. It is still factory-razor sharp. With the nickname of "pocket sword" and the look and feel of a true fighting tactical knife, it is based on the Spartan blades featured in the movie *300*. What I like about the Spartan is not only its "attitude," but that Cold Steel put some thought into its design, knowing that it is purely a fighting knife. The knife features a dual pocket clip—and this is important. The weapon is set up to be carried in your right-hand pocket, but I carry mine in my left-hand pocket, so being able to switch the clip is a great asset. The built-in "thumb plate" is also a great feature, especially when carrying the knife in the "weak hand," because you can use this thumb plate to open the knife while pulling it out of the pocket. You do this by keeping the back of the knife blade against the fabric of the pocket. The thumb plate will catch the edge of the pocket's fabric and then assist opening the knife as you draw it out of the pocket. You can also open this knife with a flick of the wrist, like I can do with my Cold Steel Voyager. The Spartan also incorporates Cold Steel's Tri-Ad locking mechanism, which is a stronger more reliable positive locking system, to ensure that the knife does not close on your fingers even under the strongest of strains against the knife in almost any given situation. This is a huge advantage when it comes to safety, especially when the knife is called into serious action.

I also like how the blade wraps around the hand, preventing the knife from slipping up the blade or off the back of the knife while being used.

The deep "belly" design of the blade allows deeper cuts and slashes, and the classic Kopis blade shape allows for the knife to be used as a stabbing weapon that ensures good penetration. Finally, the rear of the handle, or the pommel, is reinforced so that it can be used as a bludgeon in a full, "hammer fist," downward thrust or backhand/roundhouse punch to the temple. The Cold Steel Spartan is the full-on fighting knife, and that is why I carry it.

Left-Hand Pants Pocket

Normally, I do not carry anything in this pocket besides my cell phone. In some cases, I carry a 1.3-ounce can of Cold Steel Inferno pepper spray. But that is on a case-by-case basis. I do not carry anything in my left-hand, rear pocket except maybe my checkbook from time to time. In fact, it is a good practice not to carry anything in your rear pockets, especially if the openings can be viewed from behind, inviting a thief to try to mug you.

Some people carry a decoy wallet with some used gift cards, a couple of dollars, and some papers, etc.—but nothing with any ID. This is something to give an assailant, providing him reason to run off or buying you time to tactically retreat or fight.

Left Rear on the Belt

On my left rear, at about the seven o'clock position, I wear a snap-on leather key holder. Here is what I carry on my key ring: Cold Steel OC Spray, a mini flashlight, and a mini Swiss Army knife knockoff. I am a firm believer that if you are able to carry OC spray, you can never carry too much. This is why I have some on my key ring as well as carrying it in pen form.

Forbus Flashlight Carrier with Kobalt LED, 90-Lum Flashlight—At the eight-thirty to nine o'clock position on my belt, I carry a Forbus flashlight carrier with a Kobalt Tactical LED 90-lum flashlight. I saw this light at Lowe's for only thirty dollars, and it fit my flashlight carrier. I had purchased the carrier earlier for another one of my flashlights, but that one did not fit the Forbus Carrier, so I needed another. (NOTE: This is why you should keep all receipts of purchase.) I did keep the flashlight because it is a great 200-lum tactical light that I keep next to my bed as my primary flashlight.

I advise you to always carry a flashlight. There are so many needs, and someday you may be in a situation in which your life depends upon having one. A good, bright, tactical flashlight will also work as a defensive weapon: You can shine it in an assailant's eyes and temporarily blind him, allowing you to retreat. In a future that's certain to have an increasing crime rate, having multiple flashlights on your person will become critical.

Left Wrist

Casio Men's SGW100B-3V Digital Compass Twin Sensor with Green Nylon Band—Everyone needs to know what time it is, and this is a great buy at around forty dollars. This model can tell you the time locally, as well as in another global city you designate. The watch is programmed with twenty-nine time zones for forty-eight cities. I have New York City as my choice because that is the default. I need to see if it has Jerusalem; if it does, I will set it to that instead.

For us gadget geeks, this watch has some pretty neat functions, such as a digital compass. This is a great little feature—but do not look at the bezel because it can be confusing in that it always points to north. Once you have your bearings on north, you can then figure out via the bezel where east, west, and south are. From there, you can figure out where you need to go.

With dual sensors, this watch has the ability to tell the temperature, but the negative is that it takes about thirty minutes to calibrate it, and you need to have it off your wrist; otherwise, it will measure your body temperature (which isn't bad, in some cases).

It is a pretty rugged watch. I should know, because I "kill" watches all the time. I don't ever bother spending over fifty dollars on one because I know that I will eventually break it in one way or another.

This watch also has a 1/100-second stopwatch, four daily alarms, and one snooze alarm. I like the snooze alarm because I can use that when I travel as a backup to the alarm clocks in the hotel rooms. It also has an auto calendar pre-programmed until the year 2099, and a mineral, scratch-resistant glass for extra protection. Mine still does not have a scratch, so this feature works great.

Since I am getting up there in years, I also like the large LCD that is divided into three segments for a clear, easy-to-read display. Even when I do not have on my reading glasses, I can see the time. This model is also water resistant up to 660 feet, so there's no need to take it off when swimming or in the shower.

Most of all, I like the olive drab green nylon band. My other wristwatch is made by Uzi, and it has a plastic/rubber wristband. I like that watch, but the band makes my arm sweat and it is either too tight, cutting off the circulation in my wrist, or too loose, flopping all over. The Casio SGW100B is a true pleasure to wear, and you could even wear it to bed if you wanted.

Practical Advice

Becoming the gray man is an important skill to develop, especially as crime starts to rise, which it will. You will need to be equipped to protect yourself and possibly others, if needed. You will also want to blend in the background.

Above all, your goal is to get home safely on any given day. You are not some superhero; neither are you there to protect the world. You need to be ready to defend yourself if you have to, but your goal is to not have to resort to that.

And finally…

Tactical retreats, also known as running away, is totally acceptable. The only person who didn't walk away from a fight was John Wayne, and that was in the movies. You are not bulletproof or knife proof. So run, don't walk, if you think you need to get out of an area fast. Your spouse will be glad you did—and so will you.

As a last resort, always remember that it is better to face a group of twelve than it is to be carried out by a group of six. So if you have to protect yourself, fight to win, and try to make sure the other guy does not ever get up—because you will be literally fighting for your life.

chapter seven

A FEW WORDS ABOUT KNIVES

Just so that you know: I am a knife freak. I believe the guy who dies with the most knives wins. I also take carrying a knife, or multiple knives, very seriously. There are times when a knife is the best weapon to use. Sometimes just brandishing a big knife will scare off punks who think they have an easy target.

At a minimum, I carry two knives: a 5.11 tactical utility knife and a Cold Steel Spartan battle knife. I also have a Cold Steel Mini Pal, which is a one-inch push knife that I just added to my key ring; a Cold Steel Tokyo Spike that I have on a homemade carry system, riding under my right arm under my shirt; and a Cold Steel Kobun Tanto boot knife that I wear in my boot or carry on the small of my back.

I just don't think one can carry too many knives. But carrying a knife and using one are two different things. If you are going to carry a battle knife, it's important to learn some basic moves about how to use it in a fight. This is pretty simple to do. In fact, all you need to do is get some rubber knives, put chalk on them, and practice with an opponent. When you make a "cut," the chalk will leave a mark. Cold Steel sells some very good rubber practice knives that hold the chalk really well.

A Bit about Cold Steel

As you can tell, I am a big fan of Cold Steel knives. They make what I consider to be the best products for the price. Their knives are made of excellent steel that always holds its edge. They are easy to sharpen and keep sharp. But, most of all, they are affordable to the common man who needs a dependable utility knife as well as fighting knife. This is why most of my knives are Cold Steel.

Knife Blade Types

The type of knife and its shape are very important. For a utility knife, I like a drop-point blade.

Cold Steel Pro Lite drop point blade

Cold Steel Pendleton Mini Hunter

Both the Pro Lite folding lock blade and the Pendleton mini hunter are drop-point blades. They are somewhat rounded at the front end of the blade, and the cutting edge is pretty straight. This is a nice shape for day-to-day utility work; it isn't too pointed, but is pointed enough to get a job done. This knife is meant for cutting rope, twine, branches, and things like that. You can also use it for hunting, as well as for skinning and gutting an animal. This blade type does not have much of a "belly"—if it has one at all. It is a pretty straightforward knife that Grandpa would carry, or you might find it in someone's fishing tackle box.

The other blade type I like is a full-bellied blade.

Ray Gano's battle carry blade, a Cold Steel Spartan

The author's former primary battle blade, a Cold Steel Vaquero

As you can see, full-bellied blades kind of have an "S" shape to the cutting edge. This is called the "belly." This shape is specifically made for making deep, slashing cuts. As you can see in the photo, the Vaquero is also fully serrated. To be honest, I wish the Spartan was offered with this option. A serrated blade, in my opinion, is a better battle blade because it will grip and cut with less force applied, whereas a straight-edge blade needs more downward pressure to achieve effect. If an assailant happens to be wearing a leather jacket, the serrated blade will cut through this and into the skin a lot easier than would the straight-edge blade.

Why, then, am I carrying a straight-edge blade instead of the serrated? Because Spartan is that the knife that emits "attitude." When you take out that knife and open it with just a flick of the wrist, this "pocket sword" suddenly appears—with a distinctive *clack* sound—and the knife itself demands attention.

I also like how the Spartan fits the hand, the reinforced rear pommel made to crush bone, and the deep belly of the knife itself. The Cold Steel Spartan is made for one thing and one thing only: battle.

As I mentioned, I also carry my battle knife in my "weak" hand—my left hand. I am able to flick the Cold Steel Spartan open with the flick of my wrist, or I can use the tab on the back of the blade to drag along my pocket and deploy the blade exiting directly from my pocket. Again, the loud *clack* this blade makes when opening says "scary sharp" and makes quite an impression.

Learning to Knife Fight

Finding someone to spar with you using rubber knives and chalk is important, but in many cases it is not feasible. I am one such case. I live out in the "boonies"—there aren't many folks to practice with in the first place, and of the people who do live here, no one really wants to learn knife fighting. So the next best thing is DVDs—and, you guessed it, Cold Steel makes an outstanding series of DVDs on the basics of knife fighting.

The Warrior's Edge three-DVD set was the first series I purchased to learn the basics of knife fighting. The material, featuring a compilation of Lynn Thompson's knife fighting techniques, includes an introduction to long-range knife fighting, as well as instruction on guard stance and footwork, thrusts and slashes, defense, offense, training drills, and sparring.

The complete set is available for about seventy-five dollars; search the Internet for the best deals. I have converted my disks to MP4 format so that I can watch them on my iPod or telephone. I often listen to a video as I am doing chores or just relaxing outside in my chair. I also watch these videos when I want to take a break from my daily computer work. The key to learning is reinforcement and purposing in yourself what you will do in a given situation. At times, I will imagine a situation—often the parking lot at the local mega mart. Then I will go to the best portion of the video and watch that segment a couple of times pausing, replaying, pausing again, and replaying. I think of myself using those moves and imagine myself being on the screen. I play the scenario and the movie over in my head several times; sometimes, I even talk through each step.

Here's an example: I imagine that I am bending over in my car, and I hear someone yelling at me, threatening me. With my left hand, I reach for the battle knife I keep in my left cargo cell phone pocket as I am backing myself out, keeping my left side somewhat hidden from the attacker's view. I then draw my battle blade and raise it in a rearward motion as I am backing out of the car door area, allowing the blade to be flicked open with a *clack* sound. As the attacker is focusing on my left-hand blade opening and being lifted over my head, I draw my utility knife with my right hand and flick it open as well, at a lower waist position.

My attacker now sees two knives. I instantly go after his right hand, which is making threatening gestures at me. With a downward chop with my left-hand blade, I slice his right hand/wrist/arm. Then I turn sideways into a fighting stance and attack with flailing motions, cutting as fast and as many times as I can, constantly moving forward until the threat has stopped.

This is an example of talking your strategy through so that if the situation arises, you already know what you will do and how you will do it. Watching the video teaches you which actions or movements will best suit the situation. Play these over and over again in your head as you determine how you will to protect your life, the lives of your loved ones, and your property.

Part III

THE RAGING STORM

Two Weeks (?) of Literal Hell,
Then the World Settles In

chapter eight

WHEN THE STORM BREAKS LOOSE

We have talked about the coming storm, but I want to discuss what I believe will take place when the storm breaks loose. This time frame will not be very long, but it will be a time no one will ever forget. I believe it will be a time of literal hell here in the United States. This may last one or two weeks, or maybe a month. After that, the natural tendencies of man will be to bring some sort of stabilization into life. We will adapt.

The Raging Storm: How I Believe the Dollar Will Die

First of all, I am not a prophet or the son of a prophet. I am simply a watchman on the wall who has been sounding this alarm for more than five years now regarding the demise of the dollar. Many people have listened and heeded the warnings.

What you are about to read is based on historical research observing past and present situations, as well as what has happened in other countries that are currently going through or have already gone through a massive economic downfall. We are following these countries almost step by step towards implosion. I believe that in the near future, the dollar will die. We are over-leveraged to the point that a single event within the stock market can bring this nation to her knees.

Solomon, the wisest man of all times, stated that, "The thing that hath been, it is that which shall be; and that which is done is that which shall be done: and there is no new thing under the sun" (Ecclesiastes 1:9).

Man has not learned his lessons from history; therefore, he is destined to repeat the same mistakes over and over.

How It Will All Go Down

One day when nothing much is going on with the stock markets, there will be a commodities jump. Some commodity like gold or oil will spike, out of the blue. This will trigger already-programmed events, and Treasury bills (T-bills)/Treasuries will be sold off because they are the only things of value that today's fund managers have at their fingertips. They will sell off these T-bills to catch the quick chance to ride the spike and cash in on some profits.

This will set into play another series of preprogrammed events at the Federal Reserve, or the Fed. The Fed's computers, seeing these T-bills/Treasuries being sold, will snatch them up so that they can still maintain the low yields they have been manipulating in order to prevent deflation of the dollar. But the reverse will take place.

Because the Feds bought up those T-bills/Treasuries, this

will set into action other asset managers, mega banks, and other funds. They, too, will sell off their T-bills/Treasuries to get in on the Fed buying. All of a sudden, all the computer programs that have been programmed to catch the next profit margin will sell off their T-bills/Treasuries.

All of this can take place within a matter of minutes, before anyone is really aware that it is going on. When someone finally realizes what is going on, it will be too late; the lots will be cast and the damage will already be done.

At that moment, the U.S. dollar will die, and the only thing that will have been propping up the dollar—the trust and faith of the people in the currency—will also be gone. The trust and faith of the currency will have just been sold down the river, and won't be able to be recovered, no matter what the Federal Reserve, banks, or even the government will do. The death blow will have been struck, and we will have entered the path of no return.

Once all these fund managers, banks, and asset managers have sold off their T-bills/Treasuries, they will be sitting on a wad of cash. They will not buy more T-bills/Treasuries because they themselves will have lost faith in the dollar a long time ago. They will not reinvest in an already-sinking ship. In fact, they will have been praying for that one chance to dump their T-bills/Treasuries and cash them out before the dollar dies completely.

So where will these banks, fund managers, asset managers, and others put all their money? Into commodities. By the end of that incredible day, commodities of all types—precious metals, industrial metals, oil, and foodstuff—will increase exponentially.

If you see this happen, it will be your signal to go to the store as fast as you can and buy every bit of food you are able to purchase. Fill up all your cars and extra gas cans, and draw out as much cash from the bank as you can. Charge your purchases, write checks; do whatever you need to do. The dollar will have gone bust, and the world will be about to get on the "E" ticket ride on the fastest speeding train the world has ever seen.

This is the signal you need to keep a serious eye on.

Why do these things? Because ordinary people will not yet have been tipped off about what is happening. Sure, we have all lost faith in the dollar, but it will become reality when Wall Street crashes into Main Street within three to seven days after this event takes place.

Once T-bills/Treasuries are not the sure method of value as viewed by Wall Street, one question will come to everyone's mind: "Where are all those money managers going to stick all the dollars they got from selling off Treasuries?"

Will they...

A) Put the money in the bank?

B) Put the money under Aunt Flo's mattress?

C) Put the money into some overseas currency?

None of the above! They will run to what people have run to throughout history. They will start buying up commodities—the investment history has always taught is the only sure place of value for one's cash. It won't be commodity stocks, exchange-traded funds (ETFs), or bonds. These will die alongside the dollar because they are based on the value of the U.S. dollar. Anything attached to the dollar will become just as worthless. So, what we will witness is a major run on actual, hard, hold-in-your-hand commodities.

By the end of this panic-driven spiral, commodities will have risen between 50–100 percent. By week's end, we could very well be looking at an increase of 150–250 percent. All of a sudden, everyone will be looking to purchase any tangible asset that will hold value, such as gold, silver, food, or daily-use items. The prices for consumable commodities will begin to go through the roof. My personal belief is that silver will be the real skyrocket: We could very easily see silver and gold go back to a historical norm of a ten-to-one ratio. Today, gold is sitting at around fourteen hundred dollars an ounce. Ten percent of that—$140—will be the minimum for which silver will sell. But the odds are that it will sell even higher because of panic-purchasing on Wall Street. It is a very good possibility that gold could reach three thousand to five thousand dollars per ounce. This will put silver at around three hundred to five hundred dollars per ounce.

Today's price for silver per ounce is around thirty-five dollars. Compare that to three to five hundred dollars per ounce, and that is quite a return on an ounce of silver. But, at this moment, we are still primarily focusing on events taking place on Wall Street.

Once we see this commodity balloon start to go up, ordinary folks will see their first examples of hyperinflation come into play. In fact, the first place they will probably see hyperinflation is at the gas pump, when the price of gas will go up drastically overnight. I personally believe that oil will kick off all these events. If oil spikes from, say, around eighty dollars a barrel to one hundred and fifty dollars a barrel in one day, the next day, it will shoot higher and higher. Within three to five days, oil will be sitting at three hundred dollars a barrel, which is a very feasible scenario. Panic, as well as supply and demand, will cause gas to shoot up to ten, fifteen, or twenty dollars per gallon—and possibly even more. So what happens next?

Well, Wall Street will already be in a major panic; this will trickle down to Main Street. Main Street is about to wake up, and markets and prices of consumable commodities will be about to go vertical. People will storm Wal-Mart and other stores, buying up everything in sight. It will be utter chaos. Bread, noodles, camp fuel, ammo, any daily-need products will fly off the shelves.

This is why I have been advising people to store up and buy what they can now because we need to view what we are purchasing now as a hedge against inflation. For example, a week before this economic meltdown, you might be able to purchase a twenty-pound bag of rice for just twelve dollars. What will happen to that bag of rice when gas prices go to fifteen or thirty dollars per gallon? What about when the laws of supply and demand take effect?

What about when hyperinflation becomes a reality? People need to realize that hyperinflation is not "inflation" at all. *Hyperinflation is a complete breakdown in the trust of a country's currency.* Because people no longer trust their own currency, it takes more pieces of paper to purchase stuff. The currency is literally not worth the paper and ink it is printed on and with.

Here is another result that will completely wipe out many people: Because people will have freaked out and panic-bought basic commodities, their 401(k)s, IRAs, savings accounts, retirement accounts, stocks, bonds, and any other financial investments tied to the paper dollar will collapse. Sure, people may have fifty thousand to five hundred thousand dollars in one or more of these methods of saving, but when the price of a bag of rice shoots up to fifteen hundred dollars, the currency becomes pretty much worthless.

Did you know that, today, a dozen eggs in Zimbabwe—which is still in the beginning stages of hyperinflation—costs 1.3 trillion Z dollars? If a dozen eggs costs that here in the U.S. when hyperinflation hits, how much will you be able to purchase with your savings?

So even if you have a lot of dollars, the value of those dollars will be worth nothing. People who were once well off will become dirt poor overnight. Everyone will be rushing the banks to withdraw their cash so that they can turn their worthless cash into any consumable commodity that will retain its value. Here is the sequence: A spike will take place in oil, gold, or some other major commodity. Asset managers will dump their Treasuries for cash so they can catch the spike for a short profit. The Feds will rush in and buy up the Treasuries, causing a secondary sell-off from other asset managers, banks, and large corporations. The Treasury market will tank. Because of this, a few days later, stocks, bonds, and other equities will also drop in price like a lead balloon after the Treasury sell-off panic takes place.

Because all these asset managers, et al., are sitting on cash, they will need to put it somewhere safe; that will be in commodities. The price of gold, silver, oil, foodstuff, and any other commodities of value will go sky high. It is a self-perpetuating, speeding train. Nothing will be able to stop it or be able to even apply the brakes. This is where we pick up again...

Where Wall Street Meets Main Street

This speeding train coming from Wall Street will hit Main Street, and everyday people will wake up to this fact. Panic will ensue. Like the asset managers, they will dump anything they perceive to be of real-world value, but for Main Street, these real-world assets are cars, trucks, laptop computers, iPods, and even houses. All of these items will lose value in order to purchase commodities like gold, silver, food, gas, heating oil, and any sort of daily consumable need.

But, you say, gold and silver are not a daily need. You cannot eat gold and silver.

That is completely correct. But the world will still revolve around money, and this is where the natural laws of God take effect. The only true money that is God-created and ordained will rise to the surface again. It has never fallen out of favor, has always held its value, and it ALWAYS replaces devalued, depreciated fiat currency. God's only ordained and created form of money is gold and silver. What Main Street people are going to find out is that real-world assets will not go up in value in a hyperinflation scenario. They will drop.

Look at how many people have their wealth locked up in their homes. During hyperinflation, an estimated $250,000 house can easily fall to $50,000 or even less. So the good news is that if you have fifty ounces of silver, you will be able to purchase that home that has dropped to $50,000. The reason is because in a hyperinflation market, real-world assets such as cars, trucks, and even homes lose their value and pretty much become worthless, whereas fifty ounces of silver will buy just about anything you will need.

Now, if you are still reading this and you have gotten this far, you might be saying that the government will step in, Wall Street has computers to prevent this, the president will stop it, blah, blah, blah! Someone, somewhere in power, will stop this runaway train and apply the brakes to stop the hyperinflation. The answer is that no one will be able to stop it: Congress, the senate, the president, and the Fed will all be helpless. This sort of event has happened time and time again. It is all part of the fiat currency model. The first time this took place was in ancient Greece. It has also taken place in France, England, and Germany—in fact, in just about every country that has instituted a fiat currency.

Did you know that hyperinflation has taken place in the U.S. twice already? It happened once during the Revolutionary War days and then again during the Lincoln administration. In both of these times, a fiat currency was created, the people lost faith, the economy busted, and hyperinflation ensued. The government might create more laws, regulations, or quite possibly a bank holiday. It will probably try, and history shows that when the government does step in, it will always devalue the currency. It will split it so that instead of having one hundred dollars, you will have two hundred dollars. The problem is that a bag of rice costs five hundred dollars, so splitting the currency will do nothing except cause prices to shoot up even higher. Why not implement price controls? If the government is foolish enough to do this, it will whiplash back into its face and reappear as a rampant black market. The government can't fix this mess because the government is the one that caused it. So those ideas will not work.

Many conspiracy websites love to say that soldiers will be put out on the street. U.S. men and women in the military will be feeling just as much pain as we are. The military will have a hard enough time just keeping its ranks in order. You think that we will have it bad? Our men and women in the military will have it worse. Half of military families are already on food stamps; what do you think will happen when hyperinflation takes hold? Another point to remember is that our military is stretched so thin overseas that we can barely hold on to the two fighting fronts we are involved in already. In other words, there isn't enough manpower. America is too big. To utilize the military as a means of a nationwide police force basically equates to one soldier per city. Are these severely reduced forces going to be able to really do anything? No.

What about bringing in United Nations troops or foreign troops? This is another popular idea that has floated around on the conspiracy sites. Many people fail to remember that by this time, the U.S. will be a hotbed of chaos. The introduction of any foreign troops would instantly polarize the nation, and all of a sudden, the 500 million guns that are in the hands of the U.S. public would be pulled out of the closet. It would become open hunting season for any UN/foreign troop. In other words, it would be a bloodbath for anyone stepping foot onto U.S. soil. This is a fact. Give chaos a rally point, and a nationwide call to arms will naturally gravitate to it.

What about more stimulus—starting up the printing presses and injecting more money?

Can't! This is hyperinflation. People will not want the paper dollar in the first place. Commodities will be the only true asset of value. Flooding the market with even more worthless cash will not help.

What we might see—but this will take time—is to enact food/gas rationing, a return to the ration cards like they had during World War II. But, by the time this is put into effect, the people will be adapting to the New Normal and operating within a commodities-based economy. Black and gray markets will already be in effect; people will have learned how to obtain their needed items. The laws of supply and demand will have already kicked in and a New Normal economy will take effect.

So by now, all who are reading this are asking that one critical question: What do we do?

Welcome to the New Normal

The key to survival will not be surviving the nuclear bomb, it will be surviving the next day and each successive day after the bomb hits. This will be the same case when hyperinflation hits.

I used the analogy of a nuke because that is what Hollywood has portrayed. As you know by now, I do not buy into Hollywood's version of the apocalypse. Movies always show the nuke going off, then everyone "ducks and covers" as the fallout settles. Then the happy couple is seen walking off into the sunset. These movies never show what takes place after everything settles down and people adapt to a New Normal lifestyle. It will become business as usual; the rules will have just been changed. It won't be a world filled with mutant biker gangs, nor will there be bloodthirsty zombies. There will be no thermal nuclear wasteland and no empty cities. It will be nothing like Hollywood says. All we need to do is look at countries that have already succumbed to an economic disaster.

For example, look at Argentina, which had a massive economic downfall in December 2001. Its banks closed, its money devalued, and its world was turned upside down. It had a massive rise in crime, drugs, prostitution, alcohol, murder, kidnapping, theft, and muggings. Argentina went from being a first-world country to a third-world country overnight.

So how do you prepare for hyperinflation? Just do as Noah did. Build your own ark before the event takes place. But this ark is to be built of true, tangible assets—not equities, stocks, bonds, ETFs, or mutual funds. It shouldn't be built of anything that is tied to the U.S. dollar or any other foreign fiat currency. If you have been paying attention, you will have built a safety device secure enough to see you through the storm.

When the zenith of hyperinflation takes place, there will be a plethora of opportunities that you can then purchase. Robert Kiyosaki, one of my mentors, suggests purchasing cash-stream-producing residential property. He also likes mining, pharmaceuticals, industrial production, and transportation. At the height of the hyperinflation storm, these types of things will be at rock-bottom prices...pennies on the dollar.

A famous quote came from the Depression era, when the very same thing took place: "Buy when there is blood in the streets." I believe America will end up pretty much like it is today, but it will be a New Normal. We will refer to everything as being "before bank day" ("BBD") and "after bank day" ("ABD"). Crime will be higher, jobs will be scarce, and food and gas prices will be three hundred to four hundred percent higher. But we will adapt and overcome as we always have.

Another possible outcome of this that has not happened before in other countries is that we return to God. This country was founded on biblical principles; it is who we are, and it is those ideals that influence us at our core as a people. This nation always experiences a "great awakening" to God the father, the Creator of the universe, after every great financial upheaval.

Finally, turning the ship around after hyperinflation hits will take fifteen to twenty years. It took approximately twenty-five years after our last depression; it will probably take the same amount of time for us to get back on the right track after this one. Just look at Argentina; here it is 2011, and that nation is still in the throes of economic chaos. Look at Japan; it lost two decades due to its economic downfall. Did either of these countries slip into apocalyptic chaos, fall into the hands of mutant biker gangs and zombies, or turn into wastelands? No. And that will not happen here, either. What will help us speed up the healing of this nation will be a word that many people do not want to hear or accept: "sacrifice."

Will we be willing to take on three to four hard years of sacrifice so that we can emerge more quickly as a healed nation? I doubt it. But if we as a nation repent of our sins and turn back to the Lord, anything is possible. To do this, we will need strong men and women to boldly preach the gospel. Godly people will need to show that man is lost but can be saved from the fires of hell through the blood of Jesus Christ our Lord. We will need to return to being accountable to Jehovah God. Getting through this coming economic storm might be just what the doctor ordered to return this nation to what she once used to be: a good and great nation that fears God and His Son, Jesus Christ.

I am sorry to say that history shows another solution, at least in other nations. What has always come out of the economic upheaval in other nations has been a strong charismatic leader who returns (forces) the nation back to a gold- and silver-based economy.

The good of the people outweighs the good of the one.

The good of the nation outweighs the good of the family.

The state becomes its god and the dictator its high priest.

This is the solution that brought about Caesar, Napoleon, and someone else we all have heard of: Adolf Hitler. All these great leaders were born out of economic upheaval.

All led their nations to greatness quickly. All ruled with an iron fist, and all did away with dissidents who stood against them. Often, these dissidents were good men and women who maintained a moral fortitude. In most cases, they were backed up by their belief in the One True Jehovah God and His Son, Jesus Christ.

It is hard to say what the future will hold. There are so many paths that we can travel. But man, in all his wisdom, always seems to choose the path of least resistance instead of the path of good. At least that is what history has shown. The U.S. was born out of the desire for religious freedom, and that is what makes us a different nation. We have survived two other economic upheavals resulting in hyperinflation; we will survive the third. How we come out on the other side is anyone's guess. History shows that our last great awakening took place after the Civil War's hyperinflation in the late 1800s. Although many turned to the Lord in the Great Depression of the 1920–30s, it was not like the prior revival of the late 1800s.

In all of this, we, as Bible-believing Christians, will need to stand in this evil day or there is a chance that we will fall by the wayside. What will take place depends on what we do now. We can either prepare and build our arks for the sake of the gospel, or we can bury our heads in the sand and ignore the lessons of the past.

I pray that there are enough who love the Lord who will work hard to build an ark for the good of protecting and freely sharing the gospel. The other option will result in utter tyranny and oppression.

God's Word says:

"The thing that hath been, it is that which shall be; and that which is done is that which shall be done: and there is no new thing under the sun" (Ecclesiastes 1:9).

"Go to the ant, thou sluggard; consider her ways, and be wise" (Proverbs 30:25).

"The ants are a people not strong, yet they prepare their meat in the summer" (Proverbs 6:6).

"And if it seem evil unto you to serve the LORD, choose you this day whom ye will serve; whether the gods which your fathers served that were on the other side of the flood, or the gods of the Amorites, in whose land ye dwell: but as for me and my house, we will serve the LORD" (Joshua 24:15).

Part IV

THE STORM HAS HIT

Living in the New Normal

chapter nine

CRIME

You Will Need to Deal with It

In the New Normal, one thing that will become very apparent is the rise in crime. At first, it will be common, everyday crime. But it will soon become ruthless, senseless, violent crimes.

The following is a true story, recounted in my own words. This actually took place not far from where I live. In fact, my wife visited this restaurant one week to the day after this event took place.

On October 16, 1991, George Jo Hennard drove his 1987 Ford Ranger pickup truck through the front window of a Luby's Cafeteria at 1705 East Central Texas Expressway in Killeen, Texas. Once his vehicle stopped, he yelled, "This is what Bell County has done to me!" Then he opened fire on the restaurant's patrons and staff with a Glock 17 pistol, and later with a Ruger P89. The first victim was local veterinarian Dr. Michael Griffith, who ran to the driver's side of the pickup truck to offer assistance after the truck came through the window. During the shooting, Hennard approached Suzanna Hupp and her parents,

Al and Ursula Gratia. Hupp instinctively reached into her purse for her weapon, but it was in her vehicle. Because Texas did not have carry-and-conceal laws allowing honest citizens the ability to protect themselves by carrying a weapon, she could not have her gun on her person.

Her father, Al, charged at Hennard in an attempt to subdue him, but was instantly gunned down; still alive and gasping for life, he laid on the floor.

One patron, Tommy Vaughn, threw himself through a plate-glass window to allow others to escape. Suzanna Hupp, seeing her opportunity, reached for her mother, Ursula, who had been behind her—but she was not there. Looking up, she saw her mother cradling her father in her lap as Hennard walked over to her, aimed his gun inches from her forehead, and stared at her. Suzanna's mother looked up with a plea of mercy, but did not see it in the man's eyes. She then bowed her head over the head of her dying husband, and Hennard fired several rounds into the head of Ursula, killing her and finishing off her father.

Aghast and in shock, Suzanna Hupp gathered up all her energy and emotions and made for the broken window, escaping…leaving her dead parents on the floor of that Luby's restaurant.

Hennard allowed a mother and her four-year-old child to leave. He reloaded several times and still had ammunition remaining when he committed suicide by shooting himself in the head after being cornered and wounded by police.

This man stalked, shot, and killed twenty-three people—and wounded another twenty—before committing suicide. About eighty people were in the restaurant at the time.

It is this sort of senseless act of mass murder and crime that we will very possibly face on a more frequent basis when living in the New Normal.

Here is another scenario that takes place already in countries like Argentina, Bolivia, and South Africa:

A woman is alone in her house living in suburban America. It is in a nice, quiet neighborhood, the average type found in any area of the U.S.

While doing her daily tasks, the woman hears the front door-bell ring. Peeking through the peephole, she sees a young teenage girl, maybe thirteen or fourteen years old, and the poor thing is crying. "Something must be terribly wrong," the woman thinks.

She opens her front door, asks if the girl is all right, then steps through her door to approach the girl, bending to take a closer look. In a flash, the girl acts, pushing with one hand the already-out-of-balance woman against the doorframe while taking out a knife with a seven-inch-fixed blade from behind her back. She places the razor-sharp edge against the unsuspecting woman's throat.

"You move, you die," the girl says.

A few seconds later, several other teenagers appear and force the woman back into the house. They close the door and instantly start beating her up. Two teenage boys rip off the woman's clothes and start raping her right there on the living room floor. The girl and two others laugh at what is taking place and make jokes as all three watch the boys have their way with the bleeding and beat-up woman.

Once finished with their deed, the teens scour the house for valuables, taking everything they can carry without being seen. Before leaving, they all kick the woman until she is unconscious, and then they leave her for dead.

Has this happened before? Yes. But troubling is that this sort of thing will get worse in the New Normal—to the point that home invasions will become commonplace.

Don't believe me? Look at Argentina or South Africa today as the perfect examples of places where senseless, violent crime is on the increase. These sorts of events take place daily in both countries; often they are accompanied by assault, rape, and, in many cases, even murder.

This is why alarm systems are becoming ineffective; the criminals know that the homes are wired for security, so they attack when the owners are home and the alarm is off.

Before the New Normal, intruders would have to worry about defeating an alarm system. But the lack of respect for human life and the absence of morals in this nation today have created ruthless thugs. Why worry about the alarms when you can break in and have your "fun" with the occupants?

The same mentality has spawned carjacking today. Car alarms are too much of a hassle for the common thug, so why not just pull the occupant out, beat him or her to a pulp, and then take off with the car?

The real threat in a home invasion has nothing to do with the loss of a laptop, an SUV, or a diamond ring. It has everything to do with loss of life, serious injury, rape, and the additional emotional issues that many survivors and those close to them have to deal with for the rest of their lives. It doesn't have to be this way. No one should have to live as timid sheep, hoping a predator won't choose them for his next meal. While living within the New Normal, it isn't our own personal property that we need to be concerned about; we need to be concerned about our own personal safety. Protecting our property will just be the icing on the cake.

What will bring this on?

We are already seeing the beginnings of it today in America… class warfare and hatred. What will arise out of that in the New Normal is a class hatred that will encompass such senseless, violent crimes that it is hard to even describe. We need to understand that the things taking place in the United States right now are just the beginning. I hate to tell you this, but things are not going to get better; in fact, they are going to get worse—much worse.

How do I know? The Bible says so: "This know also, that in the last days perilous times shall come" (2 Timothy 3:1).

As I write this, the dollar is still wavering. It has not crashed, and hyperinflation has not taken place. Things are still somewhat sane, but we are seeing things on the outer edges of being life-changing. In the New Normal, the poor will become poorer and the middle class will be wiped out. In fact, we are witnessing the demise of the middle class already.

There is a very good chance that we will see the same thing in America that is taking place right now in South Africa: a form of experienced guerrilla criminals. Most attacks will take place at night, perpetrated by groups of three to five—maybe more, depending on how many live in the home. The criminals will already know that number, and will have lots of other information about you and your property.

The husband is usually killed in the attack. Children are sometimes tortured, depending on whether the attackers get what they want. In South Africa, you need to apply for a weapons permit, much like it is in New York and other anti-gun states.

If you are successful in obtaining a weapons permit, the bad guys will know it, and they will also know where you keep your weapon. How will they know? They get the information from the police. You see, in South Africa, those who apply for a weapons permit must give the police a full inventory and layout of the security set-up of their home.

During the New Normal, police will become severely underpaid, thus open to corruption and payoffs—much like they are in South Africa today. The police there are willing to give up information for money, and they gladly turn a blind eye. I know this because one of my Prophezine subscribers—Piet, in South Africa—gave me this information.

His is a voice speaking from the New Normal. He is living in it right now. He writes:

I am sorry if I sound angry and exasperated but I am and it is difficult to stay positive and moving forward. I cannot really tell you when last I slept like a baby. I will wake up three to four times in a night. I am always vigilant when I arrive home from work and look around to make sure the area around my house is safe to approach. You cannot let your guard down because SATAN will pounce like a lion when you are not paying attention. But I must also say that Jesus is good to us, because He keeps us safe. I keep my fitness up and HE keeps me healthy. Besides everything we still try to live a normal life.

—Piet Smit, South Africa, October 25, 2010

I learned about a story of a nine-months-pregnant woman in Buenos Aires, Argentina, who was robbed right outside the doors of a bank. She was spotted as an easy target by some thugs who were keeping an eye on the institution.

After making her withdrawal, the woman walked out of the building and was instantly approached by the thieves, who demanded the money she had just withdrawn. She willingly gave it up. But that is not all. Out of pure hatred for those who have what they themselves don't, the robbers shot the poor woman right in the face. Why? Because she had given them the money. The senseless death goes back to the class warfare taking place right now in Argentina; it is a foreshadow of things to come to the U.S.

In his paper, *On Sheep, Wolves, and Sheepdogs,* Lt. Col. Dave Grossman defined the following:

Sheep—Kind, decent people who are not capable of hurting each other, except by accident or under extreme provocation.

Wolves—The bad guys; those who feed on the sheep without mercy.

The key to surviving in the New Normal has nothing to do with being a sheep or a wolf. It has everything to do with being what Grossman calls the third option: The sheepdog. In Grossman's view, it is the sheepdog that protects the sheep from the wolves. He says that police officers are sheepdogs, although we cannot expect them to always be there to protect us. Sheepdogs are also those of us who own guns and have obtained concealed weapons permits. We are seen by the wolves of society as people they do not want to meet or deal with.

This is just the tip of the iceberg of living in and dealing with the New Normal. Establish the mindset now not to allow some ruthless thug to bring harm to you, your family, or your loved ones—much less destroy what you and your family have built, that being your home, your castle.

You MUST make up your mind right now that you will NOT allow ANY criminal to harm you or your loved ones. Determine right now that your home will NOT be broken into by ruthless criminals who would take your possessions and possibly hurt those who look to the home as shelter from the world outside.

Decide these things right now and burn them into your soul. One day, you may need to act upon this, and when you do, use extreme determination to do away with the threat until it is no longer a threat—determine it to the point of using deadly force if need be.

Purpose it, purpose it now.

chapter ten

FIGHT, FLIGHT, OR FREEZE
Purposing Your Mind

"Purposing your mind." I stated in the last chapter that this is what you will need to do, and do now. We need to make up our minds that if anyone comes upon us and means to do us harm, we must explode into action—no half-hearted attacking. When I say explode, I mean explode into a violent, unadulterated anger.

Right now, I know that I am going against many commonly held beliefs and ideals. I hate to say this, but this is the New Normal.

Here is what Scripture says:

- "Blessed be the LORD my strength, which teacheth my hands to war, and my fingers to fight" (Psalms 144:1).
- "And I looked, and rose up, and said unto the nobles, and to the rulers, and to the rest of the people, Be not ye afraid of them: remember the Lord, which is great and terrible, and fight for your brethren, your sons, and your daughters, your wives, and your houses" (Nehemiah 4:14).

- "Wherefore take unto you the whole armor of God, that ye may be able to withstand in the evil day, and having done all, to stand" (Ephesians 6:13).

I say "anger" because a person is choosing to do you harm, and you will be literally fighting for your life and for the lives of your loved ones: "But if any provide not for his own, and specially for those of his own house, he hath denied the faith, and is worse than an infidel" (1 Timothy 5:8).

If you have not determined this strategy ahead of time, your body will make the decision for you. It will choose one of three courses of action. The problem is that you do not know what choice your body will make, and because of that, the odds are against you.

What three things will your body choose from?

1. **You will fight.** This is what you *want* to do. But unless you have trained, you may not be too effective. This is why purposing it ahead of time, thinking out what you will do, training for that possibility, is very important.
2. **You will run or take flight.** This is an automatic response that you will have no control over if you are put into a situation that you have not purposed in your mind. If your body chooses this action, you may live to see another day. But what about any loved ones you may have left behind? What about your home or vehicle? What will happen to the people and property you left when you took flight? Really consider this.

3. **You will freeze.** Just like a deer that steps into the
   path of an oncoming vehicle with its headlights on,
   you will be literally frozen in fear, and your body
   will refuse to move. The odds are that if this is the
   course your body chooses to take, you will most
   likely fall prey to the one accosting you. Your family
   and property will also be in danger if you freeze.

So what is the solution? Taking the time NOW to train your
mind regarding the action you will take when your life or the lives
of your loved ones are put in danger.

For example, remember the woman who was attacked in her
own home by that gang of teenagers? Would fancy locks, a better peephole, and such have helped her? No, because she was not
aware of her situation or surroundings. She assumed that since
she was at home, no harm could come to her. She did not purpose in her mind ahead of time what she would do in case of an
attack at the front door.

This is why having the proper mindset is crucial.

For example: In Texas, it is legal for a person who holds a
carry-and-conceal license to take a gun into church. I am one of
those people. In reading the news, I have found that, at least once
a month, some crazed wacko will come into a church and start
letting bullets loose. What I have done is *purposed in my mind*
what I will do.

Every Sunday, my wife and I sit in the same place. In fact, if
you go to church, you probably do the same thing. Our church
does not have pews; it has chairs. I sit on the left end of the row,
three rows back from the front, in the left-hand side of the group
of chairs going down the middle of the church. I have chosen this

spot because it affords me a straight shot to the doors that lead into the sanctuary. These are the same doors that a person coming into the church from our front door would have to use. If a bad guy comes in, I can easily pull my gun from concealment, spin around, face the doors, and drop to one knee. While spinning, I will be getting my weapon in the ready position so that as the doors come into view, both my hands are gripping my weapon and driving it forward to fire.

Once my weapon is fully extended, I can determine whether my shooting area is safe (making sure no one is behind the bad guy), and then take the shot. I will aim for the "T" zone so that I take the perpetrator out instantly. I also purpose in my mind to shoot the "T" zone just in case the person has taken a hostage. (The "T" zone encompasses the eyebrows across the face and the line down the nose, which kind of forms a "T." If shot here, one will die instantly. The bullet will enter the front "T" zone, and will sever the brain from the spinal cord, thus stopping all brain activity to the body. The body will stop—instantly.) The perpetrator will need to see where he/she is going and will, at least, be looking over the shoulder of the possible hostage.

No matter what, I must take this shot, or else a good number of people—including a possible hostage—will be killed. I cannot hesitate. I cannot think about it. I cannot try to "talk down" the bad guy. I have perhaps a second of time to react against the bad guy and catch him off guard. If I wait any longer, he will have the upper hand, and I will probably become his first fatality. I must take the shot, and the first shot must count, or others, as well as myself, will probably die.

Do you hear the purpose in this? Can you tell that I have played this scenario over and over in my head? I have not had to do this yet, but I am fairly confident that since I have mentally rehearsed this, my brain will do as I have trained it.

Every time I step into church, I play this scenario in my mind. I act out drawing my weapon without drawing attention to myself. I spin in my chair slowly and place my right knee out so that I can place it on the ground. I play in my mind that I have taken a knee, driving my weapon forward, taking aim as I dive, clearing the area for the shot. Once all is good, I take the vital shot—all within my mind.

I will not run. I will not freeze. I will fight, and I will fight with an internal explosion, ready to do battle and defend those I love.

Now, by rehearsing this over and over again, I will be able to draw the energy and willpower to do what needs to be done. In doing this, my body is also preparing itself for battle. My body is pulling blood from it extremities and into the central core. It is producing adrenalin to feed the muscles with super-human speed and strength. Muscles are contracting, hardening up. Skin is also pulling tight and hardening. The chest and abdominal muscles follow suit; they are all getting ready to absorb a blow.

In this bodily state, my odds of surviving and continuing to fight are very good. With the wonders of modern medicine, the odds are very good that I will also survive multiple direct impacts from bullets if they are not a direct hit to the heart or the "T" zone.

By training our conscious minds, we will then set our sub-conscious minds into action when the time is called upon. But it does not stop there. We need to constantly reinforce not only our physical skills, but our mental skills as a well. By playing over and over every step we will take, we then start playing our scenario in more detail over and over again in our mind. Once that becomes cemented in, we then go into even more detail, replaying and reinforcing.

To wear the armor of God mentioned in Ephesians 6:13, we need to wear it daily so that our spiritual muscles get used to it; it will become second nature. Should the day come for us to do battle, we will have done everything we can. Once we have done all, then we must stand for what is right, taking action to protect.

Developing the Purpose and Mindset

How can you train yourself to go from a state of everyday life (peace) to an explosive fury (war) without warning? How do you gain that attacking/defensive attitude?

It comes from training.

Initial Training on Your Own

By training on your own, one of the strongest things that you will do is build confidence. When your confidence is built, there is little hesitation to act in an attacking, defensive attitude. You know you have the training, tested your ability, and experienced—to a point, all in your mind—a variety of potential situations.

It does not matter how old or how young you are. Do you know that King Leonidas was sixty years old at the battle of Thermopylae? This is the same Leonidas who was portrayed in the movie *300*. The famous Greek phrase *Molon labe!* ("Come and take them!") was given in response to Xerxes demand that the Spartans surrender their weapons at the Battle of Thermopylae.

It corresponds roughly to the modern equivalent of the English phrases "over my dead body," "bring it on," or, most closely, "come and get it."

Start Training Now

You are never too old to do some form of training, especially if you have a family to protect. One of the easiest ways to train yourself is by standing in front of a mirror and SLOWLY going through the reach, draw, and deployment of your weapon from concealment, then re-holstering it.

This may be pepper spray, a stun gun, a knife, or a firearm. It does not matter. What matters is that you do this in front of a mirror so that you can see yourself making each individual movement.

So let's start.

Reach, draw, and deploy. Assuming that you are right-handed, you and your weapon are at the approximate 3:30 position on your body.[20] Reach back and place your hand on your weapon.

If you are wearing a shirt for concealment, use the left hand to pull your shirt up and out of the way so that your right hand can obtain a good grip on the weapon. If your shirt or jacket is loose-fitting and you can easily obtain your weapon, then practice doing this with your right hand alone.

This is your **reach.** Practice this about fifteen or twenty times, doing it slowly.

Next, reach and then **draw** your weapon, again doing this fifteen to twenty times, slowly.

Next, reach, draw, and **deploy** your weapon—again doing this about fifteen to twenty times, slowly.

This is boring and repetitive, but it trains your muscles to do the same thing over and over again. The goal is to be able to reach for your weapon, draw, and then deploy it without ever thinking.

When you are practicing your reach, draw, and deploy as you watch yourself in the mirror, be critical of your actions, making sure you do the same thing over and over again.

If you practice this every day for about fifteen to thirty minutes a day— seriously, thinking of nothing else, remaining completely focused—for a whole week, by the week's end you will be amazed at the skill you have developed. In fact, by the end of the week you will be amazed at how fast you can reach, draw, and deploy your weapon.

Give it a try, and see. I know that I was amazed at what some fifty-year-old guy can do. It is all about training the muscles and reinforcing muscle memory.

Muscle Memory?

In the movie *Karate Kid*, a character named Mr. Miagi, the teacher, tells his pupil to wax a car. Mr. Miagi demonstrates how to apply the wax in a circular motion with his left hand and how to take it off in a circular motion with his right.

All day, the boy is putting wax on…and taking wax off. He ends up cleaning and waxing several cars. By the end of the day, he is dead tired, and is wondering why he did all that work when all he wanted to do was learn karate.

Then, all of a sudden, Mr. Miagi threw a punch at the pupil, and without even thinking, the boy used the "wax off" motion to deflect the punch. A second punch came in on the left side; and the pupil used the "wax on" motion to deflect the punch.

This is an example of muscle memory. In training your reach, draw, and deploy, you are creating muscle memory—your own form of "wax on...wax off."

Make sure that you continue to practice this every day for at least ten to fifteen minutes a day. Remember that if you do not practice, your muscle memory will digress, and you will lose the skill. So, constant reinforcement is needed.

The mirror is also your best training aid. Watch yourself take each "step" in deploying your weapon. Perfect and refine your reach, draw, and deploy. The milliseconds you can shave off of your action will be a huge factor in a street fight.

Taking It a Step Further

Go through the motion of using the weapon. If you are using pepper spray, practice spraying it. This is when an inert, dummy pepper spray comes in handy. Practice aiming at your face in the mirror, and attack. Once you have attacked, look left and right for possible other bad guys. Imagine that you may have to take them on. Point your pepper spray where you look. If you look left with your head, your hand will follow. The eyes and hands become one single piece, much like a turret on top of a tank. Where you look, your hands with your weapon will instantly follow.

Once you have deemed the coast clear, re-holster/put away your weapon in the very same slow, methodical motion you used to bring the weapon out.

You may be asking: Since the fight is over, why practice putting the weapon away? You may have to put your weapon away in a hurry so that you can run away, go for help, or assist a friend or loved one.

After engaging in a fight for your life, you will be in a form of shock. People who do not practice putting away their weapons often drop their weapons right in front of them after the fight.

You've probably seen the old Western movies where there is a shootout in the street and the winner, who is all glossy-eyed, looks down at that Colt pistol and then drops it. This is what literally happens. The body is in shock, the mind has shut down, and you are flying on autopilot until you come to your full senses again.

FYI…if you are in a fight for your life and you win, which is the goal, the odds are, after holstering your weapon, you will probably throw up. This is a common occurrence after such a dose of adrenalin, because you are "coming down" from the fight. Another common physical response after a fight is shivering—you may temporarily lose use of fine motor skills. Again, this is your body reacting to the large dose of adrenalin that is still in your system.

Interestingly, during a fight, you will probably experience loss of hearing, tunnel vision, and possibly the perception that time or the world is slowing down—or that you are moving at an extremely fast speed. All of these are ways your body deals with the large amounts of adrenalin it has injected into your system in preparing to fight. Since your body is now in shock, you are purely acting on instinct. If you haven't trained your body to re-holster, you will do just as they do in the movies: drop your weapon right where you stand. The odds are that you will not even know you dropped it; in fact, you will probably have some sort of minor panic attack moments later because your weapon is not on you. You will swear that you still had it in hand or on your body.

After a fight like this, the next instinct will be to attend to your family and loved ones, or to back off and get away from the area—in other words, retreat. So, always practice a slow and methodical re-holstering of your weapon. Train the muscle memory so that when the time comes, your body will go into autopilot and re-holster your weapon on its own—without your thinking about it.

What if more bad guys happen to be in the area? You will be prepared to defend yourself and your loved ones again.

If your primary weapon is a knife, practice deployment and attack until the threat is stopped. Then check for more bad guys and re-holster. If you're using pepper spray or a stun gun, do the same thing. Do this over and over again, making sure that you are doing the same thing time after time.

Once you have done this to the point of boredom, do it about ten more times, creating that "muscle memory." Whatever defensive/attack mode you choose, get super sharp at using it. Now, you have prepared yourself for that "evil day," and in having done so, you will "stand" and be ready to do battle.

There are a variety of ways to train for purpose and mindset.

Taking Classes, Watching Videos, Training with Others

I find that variety helps sharpen the purpose and mindset, ensuring that you are constantly learning and improving. You can introduce variety by taking a formal class, purchasing a DVD series, or even watching a TV show. No matter what, having some sort of outside influence will help improve and hone your skills.

I am fortunate to have several gun ranges in my area offering certified classes, as well as group training and special sporting events. One such group event is called the International Defensive Pistol Association, or IDPA.

The International Defensive Pistol Association (IDPA) is the governing body of a shooting sport that simulates self-defense scenarios and real life encounters. It was founded in 1996 as a response to the desires of shooters worldwide. The organization now boasts membership of more than 17,008, including members in fifty foreign countries. One of the unique facets of this sport is that it is geared toward the new or average shooter, yet is fun, challenging and rewarding for the experienced shooter.

The founders developed the sport so that practical gear and practical guns may be used competitively.

An interested person can spend a minimal amount on equipment and still be competitive. The main goal is to test the skill and ability of the individual, not equipment or gamesmanship.

"Competition only" equipment is not permitted in this sport.[21]

At our gun range, we have a local chapter of the IDPA called Texas Tactical.

Here is what the Texas Tactical website says:

The Texas Tactical club is an IDPA affiliated club which conducts matches for both handguns and carbine formats. All skill levels are welcome to participate. This type of shooting does not require expensive specialty gear or weapons. Street practical equipment and techniques are all that is needed. These matches are extremely well attended. New shooters are required to attend safety orientation, so come early your first time out.[22]

Carbine (close-quarters combat range) matches are held on the first Saturday of each month, and the IDPA handgun matches are held on third Saturday and fourth Sunday of each month.

So, if you have twenty-five dollars and about 150 rounds, you can go out and challenge yourself to real-world scenarios like you see on TV. On top of this, you spend a great day at the range with like-minded people—and you will probably walk away with a few names and phone numbers to boot.

When you think about it, the cost factor versus what you gain is a win-win situation.

But what about knife fighting?

Well, I already mentioned Cold Steel's *Warrior's Edge* DVD series. This is a good beginning series that is well worth the money.

Another source of great DVD training is through a company called One Source Tactical (www.onesourcetactical.com). This is a sub-company of Suarez International, described as "reality-based, student-focused, concepts-driven, and combat proven."

This is a good place to talk about tactical training academies and schools. These schools teach and train military and police tactics as well as situational offense and defense. Classes are normally offered in handguns, shotguns, tasers, mace/pepper spray, hand-to-hand combat, and even knife fighting. Some of these schools may also offer classes in obtaining your carry-and-conceal firearms license, and if they do, I highly recommend applying.

Tactical training classes are the ones I tend to gravitate toward because they offer real-world training from experienced instructors—usually former police officers, military special operations, and members of special forces. Because I was once in special-ops, I am drawn to this type of on-the-street/real-world training. To put it simply: It is what I am used to and what I was brought up with during my time in the U.S. Army.

Suarez International offers classes all over the United States at reasonable prices. Not only does the company offer classes on handguns and rifles, but it is one of the few that presents knife training as well as open-hand/hand-to-hand training. Once you graduate from the basics, you can also take classes like Extreme Close Range Gun-Fighting.

Here is a brief description of this class:

> We cover many of the topics only hinted at in CRG [close-range gun-fighting], such as shooting from seated positions (i.e., in a vehicle), fighting when injured, and a dynamic module of instruction dealing with the ultra-close 0-6' distance. We also introduce fundamental gun vs. knife concepts. Most importantly, in this course we introduce the student to the dynamic and chaotic world of force-on-force Interactive Training.
>
> Through a series of carefully executed and designed drills, the student will get the opportunity to apply what they've learned against live role-players. This is as close as you can get to a real gunfight without risking your life.[23]

One of the main reasons I like Suarez International is that Gabe Suarez, the owner, is a Christian and runs an ethical business based on godly principles. In fact, here is what Gabe says on the company's "About" page:

The Bottom Line

The training that Suarez International provides, has its basis in the martial systems of both the east and the west, and both from the past and the present. Students are taught how to think as well as how to fight, and by extension, how to win a fight, not merely how to shoot at a "target" or how to make a "technique" work in a [soft matted gym or] dojo. We are committed to make you a better combatant. I hope you enjoy viewing our website and we hope to train with you very soon. Regardless of your occupation, it's my sincere prayer that the Lord will Bless you, strengthen you and watch over you in your endeavors. "Blessed be the Lord my rock who trains my hands for war and my fingers for battle." ~ Psalm 144:1[24]

I plan on taking my advanced training with Suarez International, and I have gotten involved with a local training group here in the Texas hill country that focuses on knife and weapons fighting. Many in the group are also Suarez International graduates. I highly recommend this company not only for knife training, but for personal protection training as a whole.

If you are not able to take training with Suarez International, many other fine academies are out there. If you have multiple police agencies in your area, the odds are that you have some sort of tactical training school in your vicinity as well. To find out, do what many people do and just Google "tactical training schools" as well as your area and you should come up with some names. Or, try the old-fashioned way and check your local yellow pages. Most tactical schools are usually endorsed by the National Rifle Association and the IDPA, as well as other recognized gun organizations. If you are a member of one of these, contact them to point you in the right direction of a good school.

If you have a college nearby, there is also a very good chance that you have a local Society for Creative Anachronism (SCA). Here is how the group describes itself:

> The Society for Creative Anachronism [www.SCA.org] is an international, non-profit, educational society celebrating pre-seventeenth century history. It has members who study every aspect of medieval life. We are brewers, archers, calligraphers, heralds, fencers, spinners, blacksmiths, costumers, dancers, cooks, and armored fighters. We enjoy feasting, spinning, needlepoint, equestrian, leatherwork, beadwork, socializing, live weapons competition, period music, theatre, and much more. If someone did it back then, you can bet someone is trying to do it now.[25]

The goal is to learn through doing, and sharing one's subject knowledge with others. The SCA encourages historical research and recreation, and most importantly, preserving a code of conduct, a mentality, and philosophy that in many ways is lacking in the modern world.

Knife fighting, short sword, and even rapier skills can all lend themselves to helping you obtain knife fighting skills that can be transferred to the need to defend yourself on the street.

In fact "heavy list fighting" or "rattan stick fighting," practiced in the SCA, is a unique art also considered as an official martial art. In place of actual weapons, rattan—which is looks something like bamboo—is used to construct a wide array of weapons such as swords, axes, spears, mace, poll-arms, the great sword, daggers, and other hand-held weapons used by the SCA armored fighters during combat.

If there is an SCA group in your area, it will usually hold weekly sword/battle training. There is always a dedicated marshal of arms there, one who has learned to wield the blade very effectively. In the SCA, you "battle" your way to the top, just as in the days of old. Those who have obtained names, ranks, and even positions of "royalty" do so via the field of battle.

As a side note, getting involved with the SCA is a lot of fun, too. If you have ever been to a Renaissance Fair, that is what it is like—except the SCA meets more often, has more tournaments, and at times even gets together to just have one big battle or "war" for bragging rights in the SCA realm. You can learn more about the SCA at http://www.scademo.com.

Finally, a place you can look to obtain knife fighting skills are Mixed Martial Art (MMA) gyms. Many MMAs offer Filipino knife and stick fighting. Mixed Martial Arts are becoming more and more popular, and the goal of MMA is just out-and-out street fighting. This form of martial arts stems from the Saturday wrestling matches many of us used to see on TV when we were growing up. Remember all those "cage bouts" that Roddy Piper and Andre the Giant fought? Well, MMA took the cage fight and expanded on the idea. Much of MMA focuses on Brazilian jujitsu, which is more of a form of grappling or fighting on the ground mixed with Filipino kick boxing. Integrate some tae kwon do or Korean karate, Jeet Kune Do, Wing Tsun, and kung fu, and you have the basis of Mixed Martial Arts.

To help whittle down your choices, look for schools that teach the AMOK! Knife fighting from Tom Sotis. This is an internationally known system and can easily be found.

Here's some information about Tom and AMOK!:

In 1992, Tom Sotis established the International Blade Fighters Guild and founded AMOK!, with knife work becoming his sole occupation since. Fifteen years and twenty-plus countries later, Sotis' reputation as one of the top combat instructors in the world was hard-earned, and he continues training people in some of the world's most dangerous places. Sotis' seminars and camps attract students and instructors of all levels from shooters, fighters, martial arts, and from other weapons systems. Tom enjoys a lifestyle of adventure, travel, spreading knife culture, and making new friends.[26]

The AMOK! knife fighting system is a good standard, and if you can find an accredited school, you know that you are getting good solid training.

Now a note of warning: I do not endorse studios that incorporate any form of religious practice associated to some of the eastern martial arts. This is why I tend to stick with organizations like Suarez International, SCA, AMOK!, and places that teach dedicated knife fighting systems. If you can find a martial arts studio that will offer purely weapons training, then that is a good thing and you are blessed to do so. Often the religious aspect of the eastern martial arts will sooner or later creep in if you are not cautious.

I know I've included a lot here focusing on physical security, home, and self protection, but this is going to be critical to know when the New Normal takes place. It will not matter how much food or cool stuff you have if you are unable to protect it because it will be taken from you and probably at the cost of serious injury or possibly even death.

COMING SOON

Surviving and Thriving after the Coming Storm

We have reached the end of this book, but many of you are asking, "What about food?" I will pick up where this book leaves off with a second in the series, tentatively titled *Surviving and Thriving after the Coming Storm.* In the next book, I will focus primarily on procuring food, growing food, fishing, and hunting in the city, as well as bartering, cash, and the economy in the New Normal.

To give you a little taste, here is a sampling of material from that book.

City Foraging: Edible Begonias?

Begonias, the world's most common houseplant, are edible. They are one of the most common bedding plants for three reasons: they look great, they like the shade, and deer don't like to eat them.

Most city dwellers don't know begonias are edible. If you are walking around your neighborhood and taking an inventory of what your city has to offer, you will probably see begonias in abundance. That is why I have decided to list them as one of the plants you need to identify and mark on your local map or GPS waypoint.

What is interesting is that in fancy grocery stores, it is becoming fashionable to have flower petals in your soup and salad, or as a garnish. Often, the petals are those from none other than begonias.

Plant the wax begonia, the most common variety of begonia, in your yard. For those who live in an apartment, the plants thrive in pots and containers. People will admire them, but very few, if any, will know that they are part of this week's dinner menu.

At least fifteen types of begonia are edible:

B. annulata (aka B. hatacoa)
B. auriculata
B. barbata
B. gracilis
B. grandis var evansiana (use sparingly due to its medical uses)
B. hernandioides
B. malabarica
B. mannii
B. picta
B. palmata
B. plebeja (stems peeled, sap is used to make a drink)
B. semperflorens
B. rex and B. roxburghii (cooked)

Begonias are a common part of mealtime in countries such as Mexico, India, and Brazil. Basically, wherever they grow, they have been a food source to people in the know. So welcome to the club of being in the know.

Begonias have been found to be a good source of vitamin C, and were often consumed by the pirates of the Caribbean to prevent scurvy. Well, I threw in the pirate stuff because the plants are native to Central and South America. They are also native to Japan, India, Indonesia, Burma, and most of Asia, and all the way to South Africa. Pretty much wherever there is a semi-humid environment along with warm weather, you will find begonias.

In Japan, begonias are eaten like we would eat steamed spinach: Throw them in a pot, add some salt, pepper, and water, and you have a side dish. In Indonesia, they are used to make a sauce for meat and fish because of their tart taste. They are also used to make salads from China to Brazil. Pretty much anytime you would make greens cooked or raw, you can substitute those for begonias.

Begonias contain oxalic acid, which can make them rather tart at times. In high concentrations, oxalic acid is a dangerous poison, but such immediately toxic levels are not found in foodstuffs; rather, they are found in the industrial arena, in some bleaches, anti-rust products, and metal cleaners, among other things. As I have mentioned, it is also a naturally occurring component of plants, like begonias and other dark green, leafy foods.

Also, because begonias are ground cover, make sure to forage from plants that have not been treated with pesticides and sprays. And, as with any edible plant, make sure that you have clearly identified it. When in doubt, don't eat it.

Begonias have been harvested and eaten for at least fourteen hundred years. From what I understand, China has the earliest records of eating begonias, using *begonia grandis*. There, it was used as an herbal medicine, as an astringent to clean wounds and reduce swelling, and to treat a number of diseases. A great website to visit and learn more about begonias is http://www.begonias.org.

City Foraging: The Prickly Pear Cactus

Opuntia (OH - pun - tea - ya), or the prickly pear cactus, is the most common of the edible cacti found here in the U.S. It is native to every state except Maine, New Hampshire, and Vermont. Hawaii did not have any until it was recently introduced and naturalized. Believe it or not, opuntia is also native to southern Alaska; so yes, it even grows in the Great White North, too.

Besides being edible, the blossoms of the prickly pear will greatly benefit your garden by attracting bees, butterflies, and hummingbirds. This is beneficial because the bees and butterflies help pollinate the other plants in your area.

You can eat the pads of the cactus pretty much year-round. But it is the prickly pear fruit that most people are familiar with. You can tell they are ripe when they turn deep red to purple. Here in Texas, the fruit starts to show on the plant around July, ripening in August, and continuing to produce fruit almost all summer and fall. In fact, a large cactus can put off hundreds of fruit during the season.

How to Harvest

The opuntia has "glochines." I call them "gotchas." These are microscopic thorns/hairs that remind me of really small slivers. They grow in clusters on the cactus pad, but you can pull them out with tweezers, or many people say that duct tape also works. They do come out pretty easy, but they are a still painful.

To remove the glochines from the plant, rinse them off with running water or burn them off with a propane torch (or even a candle). You can also peel the fruit while wearing tough leather gloves, but I like to remove the thorns first, then wash before peeling. I want to make sure I have gotten all those little glochines off the fruit—not for fear of eating them, but because it's easy to get tired of the little "gotchas" they give while working with them. Pick the fruit with VERY heavy leather gloves or long kitchen/barbecue tongs. This way, you don't come in contact with these little thorns.

To harvest the pads, all you do is grab a pad and they break off pretty easily. You can also use a knife and cut them off from the base or trunk of the cactus. They are pretty easy to harvest. The pads also have the small glochines, but they surround a large long thorn. They wash off using a hose, so that helps in the harvest. Once you pick them, you can also burn off the thorns and then peel the outside of the pad with a knife or peeler.

How to Eat Opuntia—Prickly Pear

Holding the football-shaped fruit, cut it in half, lengthwise. This will expose the red flesh and seeds. You can eat the fruit raw or cooked. When fully ripe, it has a raspberry/pear/kiwi-like flavor. Be sure to remove the seeds with a spoon because they are very hard and can break your teeth.

Do not throw away the seeds. Remember, this is city foraging, so we use what we gather. As you clean the seeds from the fruit, let them fall into a fine strainer and wash them off. Put these seeds in your food dehydrator. Once dried, they can be milled into flour.

Once you have cleaned the fruit, you can eat it fresh, or you can make jams and jellies, syrups, and fruit juice concentrate. You can even dehydrate the fruit into fruit leather (fruit "roll-ups"). Pretty much anything you can use standard fruit in, you can substitute with opuntia's prickly pear.

As for the pads, once you have them cleaned and peeled, there are several ways to eat them. Brush on some olive oil, salt, pepper, and garlic, then grill. When they turn sage green or become pretty floppy, they are done. Or plate them as a side dish, sliced lengthwise or served whole. You can also dice them, then boil with onion, garlic, salt, and pepper until they turn from bright green to sage green.

When preparing the pads, you will notice they emit a slimy juice—much like okra. This is normal, but some folks don't like the texture, so you can just wash this away. Once you have washed and strained the pads, put them in a bowl with some chopped green onion, cilantro, tomato, finely diced, pickled jalapeño peppers (optional), lime juice, lemon juice, salt, pepper, and any other spices you like, and you have made a really refreshing, great-tasting salad.

To step it up a notch, add some raw shrimp and a sturdy white fish like snapper. The lime and lemon juice will "cook" the fish, turning it into ceviche. This will take about two to three hours of marinating in the cactus salad—which will also allow time to infuse the salad with more flavor.

You can also cut the pads into thick, long strips and pickle them. You will find them prepared this way and sold as *napolino* or *napales* in the Mexican food section of stores. Get a jar and give it a try; it is really good. I can eat a whole jar in a day. If you like pickles, you will like this.

Please know that opuntia is good for you. Some studies have shown that it lessens low-density cholesterol. It is low in calories and sodium, and high in fiber and vitamin C. It also helps control blood sugar.

Cautions

Besides avoiding the spines, which seems pretty obvious, never eat any part of any cactus that has white sap. If the cactus you are picking has white sap, you do not have opuntia, but some other cactus.

City Foraging: A Reminder

The opuntia is easily found, and often people won't think to harvest it. Do not make it obvious that you are harvesting this plant. Consider harvesting when people's activity is low—possibly at night. It is natural for people not to consider this plant as a food source. This is mainly due to the hassle from the thorns and glochines. So this is a plus for you, in that it will give you a good food source during lean times.

Your City Foraging Map

We have gotten our books on local plants that we can eat, we have done our research, and we have even planted some of these plants in our own yard, knowing that most people will not recognize them as a food source.

Next, we need to broaden our scope and shopping list, and conduct some recognizance to discover what other edible plants are in our area. Equipped with the right information, you will be surprised at how much you will be able to find.

So let's get started.

You will need a map of your local area. You want a rather close-up map showing your area in detail. The best places to get that are Google Maps at http://maps.google.com and Google Earth at http://www.google.com/earth/index.html. With both of these, you can create a rather detailed map of food sources in your neighborhood.

Using Google Maps

First you need to create a Google account so that you can save your maps. Once you have a Google account, you can create as many maps as you want. For example, let's create a map for prickly pears.

Go to Google Maps and enter your address. When you do this, chances are that it will take you right to your house or a few houses down. Next, switch to the "satellite" mode, and you will be able to look down—with a bird's-eye view—on where you live. You will probably be able to see your car and, if you have pets, you may see them as well.

A Note on Privacy

Yes, this seems very "big brother," but this is the age of "big brother." The key is to learn to adapt and overcome. Learn to be a small blip on the radar; that's what we are trying to teach through this book.

Many are concerned with privacy when using sites such as Google Maps and Google Earth. If you have access to the Internet and have ever set up an email account, there is already a "folder" of information about you, and all the credit bureaus and the government have access to this information. They already know what you had for breakfast, and they know the odds for whether you will eat in or go out for dinner. So to balk and say you will not get a Google account is foolish (that is, unless you know of some other free mapping source that has as many capabilities as Google Maps and Google Earth). This is about feeding yourself and your family when everyone else is in competition for the same food sources. You need every advantage you can get in this literal dog-eat-dog world of the New Normal.

Now back to where we were.

The Prickly Pear Map

As an example, I have opened a Google account, entered my address, and saved the map as PRICKLY PEARS. You can see in the photo that I have put a description in with the map—and I have also made the map UNLISTED. THIS IS IMPORTANT. If you do not want everyone in your area knowing of your food source maps, then make the map UNLISTED. The nice thing is that you can also share these maps with your networked prepper group/tribe if you choose to do so. All you need to do is share the URL with those you wish to allow access to this map.

Once you have a saved map, you can start marking the locations of prickly pears in your general vicinity. Using your mouse, you can left click—you will see the mouse change into a fist, as if it is grabbing the page. Next, pull the map in the direction you want to go and you will come to your first prickly pear source.

Google map marking a prickly pear cactus bush location

As you can see, I have identified my first Prickly Pear bush. Using a blue marker from the upper left corner, I dragged it to where the plant is located. I then titled it "Prickly Pear bush #1." You can put any sort of description here that you want. For example, if there are dogs nearby that might bark, note that. If the people who own the bush are hostile, note that. Note how big the plant is and the date of the last time you saw the plant. There is always a chance that something like this will get torn up or eaten. If this happens, do not kill the location. Plants such as the prickly pear will spawn off new growth and there will be young, tender pads in the same location the following spring. These are excellent to eat.

Next, left click and drag the map to your next location, where you can identify the next prickly pear bush. Give it a name, such as "Prickly Pear bush #2," hit OK, and it will be saved to your map. Continue to do this with all your other food sources, creating new maps for each additional one.

If you have Google Earth, which is free to download, you can do the same thing. (For those concerned about privacy, you can use Google Earth without having to set up a Google account.). You can save your maps right there on your computer, but you will need access to the Internet so that Google Earth can download the maps of the area you are inquiring about. Google Earth works the same way Google Maps does, but it offers more features. For example, you can create routes for walking or driving from plant to plant. I personally like the features that are in Google Earth, and if you have a GPS such as Garmin or Magellan, you can import your Google Map information into your GPS.

Using USGS Maps

If you want to get farther away from online resources like Google Maps and Google Earth, you can go to the U.S. Geological Survey's website (http://topomaps.usgs.gov/) and order maps of your local area.

This is where I get physical maps of our area. A 1:24,000 scale should do, but if you can get even closer, that is better. You can walk your area with your map and mark the food plants you find. This is kind of the old-fashioned way, but it serves the purpose. Another source of maps is your local gas station, which often offers advertising maps that are closer in scale and easier to mark.

Using a GPS

If you are a "techie" like I am, using a handheld GPS with software is a great way to record all the food sources in your area. In fact, for those who are concerned with privacy, using a GPS is the best way to go. Just go around your neighborhood and mark waypoints to all the cacti and other edible plant sources. This allows you to determine the location and the best time to harvest a little bit from each plant so that others do not notice it is being picked. Mapping this out will help you in your harvest and prevent you from overharvesting a food source.

Once you have your food sources marked, download the information to your computer, where you can zoom in, make notes, create routes, and note harvest times, etc. The key in keeping these records is maintaining a renewable resource.

The goal in all of this is to help you not to get "picked off" from other people who see you gathering and foraging in the city. The more random you can make your food-gathering expeditions, the more food you will be able to harvest.

One more thing to do with your mapping resources is note the optimum harvesting time for each plant. If you have a short harvest time, then you will want to take full advantage of the food sources.

For example, in our area, pecans start dropping around September or October. If that's the case where you live, you should mark that in your mapping software so that you are prepared to gather as many pecans as you can for a food source and for storage. Research food sources such as this well ahead of time, because you will be in competition with others for this valuable resource. Finding out ahead of time where the trees are located and when the pecans ripen, and determining the proper means to harvest and bag up your gatherings will help you become as efficient as possible. Having gloves and canvas bags with straps, and becoming proficient at using picking tools like a long-arm apple picker, a rolling pecan/nut picker, and other such items will ensure effectiveness in your city foraging.

NOTES

1   Wikipedia contributors, "1989 Loma Prieta Earthquake," *Wikipedia,* http://en.wikipedia.org/w/index. php?title=1989_Loma_Prieta_earthquake&oldid=426476814.

2   EMP is caused by a low-level nuke blast taking place in the atmosphere. The resulting surge of magnetism will disable all electronic devices.

3   Wikipedia contributors, "Fiat money," *Wikipedia,* http://en.wikipedia.org/w/ index.php?title=Fiat_money&oldid=427645908.

4   Henry Campbell Black, *Black's Law Dictionary,* 6th ed. (West Group, 1991).

5   Daniel L. Abrahamson, "Iranian Oil Bourse Opens for Business: A Final Step toward U.S. Dollar Collapse & Preemptive Nuclear Strike," *Infowars,* May 9, 2006, http://www.infowars.com/articles/economy/iranian_oil_bourse_opens_ for_business.htm.

6   "52 Must Read Quotes from Legendary Investor Warren Buffett," *Investing School,* http://investing-school. com/history/52-must-read-quotes-from-legendary-investor-warren-buffett/.

7   Adapted from Robert T. Kiyosaki and Sharon L. Lechter, *Rich Dad's Prophecy: Why the Biggest Stock Market Crash in History Is Still Coming... and How You Can Prepare Yourself and Profit from It!* (Reed Business Information, 2002).

8   Ibid.

9   Mary Williams Walsh, "Social Security to See Payout Exceed Pay—In This Year," *New York Times,* March 24, 2010, http://www.nytimes.com/2010/03/25/ business/economy/25social.html.

10   "Obama Shatters Spending Record for First-Year Presidents," *Fox News,* November 24, 2009, http://www.foxnews. com/politics/2009/11/24/obama-shatters-spending-record-year-presidents/.

11   Sebastian Moffett and Alkman Granitsas, "Crisis Deepens; Chaos Grips Greece," *Wall Street Journal,* May 6, 2010, http://online.wsj.com/article/SB1000 1424052748703961104575225472577513414.html.

12   Tim Gerber, "Convicted Child Molester Arrested in Stabbing; 46-Year-Old Juan Leandro Villareal Charged With Aggravated Robbery," KSAT 12 News, July 26, 2010, http://www.ksat.com/news/24391637/detail.html.

13   Nicholas J. C. Pistor, "Layoffs to gut East St. Louis police force, *St. Louis Today,* July 30, 2010, http://www.stltoday.com/news/local/illinois/article_dfb230c2- 9bf3-11df-9731-0017a4a78c22.html.

14   Ashlie McEachern, "Flu Threat Rises; 100 New Cases in New Braunfels, TX," *Herald-Zeitung,* April 30, 2009.

15   www.excaliburdehydrator.com.

16   Peggy Trowbridge Filippone, "Canned Milk History—Evaporated and Sweetened Condensed Milk," About.com, http://homecooking.about.com/od/milkproducts/a/canmilkhistory.htm.

17   Jeremy Morgan, "Venezuela Attempts Gun Control by Limiting Bullets," *Latin American Herald Tribune*, http://laht.com/article.asp?ArticleId=344534&CategoryId=10717.

18   Edecio Matrinez, "Craigslist Diamond Ring Ad Leads to Father's Murder in Home Invasion, Say Wash. State Cops," CBS News, http://www.cbsnews.com/8301-504083_162-20004553-504083.html.

19   Wikipedia contributors, "AK-47," *Wikipedia,* http://en.wikipedia.org/w/index.php?title=AK-47&oldid=427111574.

20   Note: The 3:30 position: If you are looking forward, your body is 12:00 and your right hip is 3:00. Then, just behind your right hip will be the 3:30 position. This is the favored position to carry most weapons because your right hip will conceal a gun, knife, stun gun, pepper spray, etc.

21   International Defensive Pistol Association, http://www.idpa.com/.

22   Texas Tactical, "IDPA Matches," http://www.texastactical.net/matches/idpa.asp.

23   Suarez International, http://www.suarezinternationalstore.com/extremecloserangegunfighting.aspx.

24   Ibid.

25   Society for Creative Anachronism, http://www.scademo.com/.

26   Amok! Combatives, http://www.amokcombatives.com/.